ADRIA[illegible] D

TRUE CRIME CANADA

REAL CANADIAN CRIMINAL CASES

Imprint

Authors: Adrian Langenscheid, Sarah Fischer, Laura Regenauer, Lisa Bielec, Marie van den Boom, Saskia Rademacher, Chenoa Dittberner

ISBN: 978-3-98661-038-8 Paperback
ISBN: 978-3-98661-037-1 Hardcover

Editing: Stefanie Löschmann, Hannah Thier, BA, MSc., Daniela Bertram
Translation: Lea Prescher

1st edition January 2022

Printing house: Amazon Media EU S.á r.l., 5 Rue Plaetis, L-2338, Luxembourg
Cover image: © Canva (canva.com)
Cover design: Pixa Heros, Stuttgart

Some dialogues and statements of the persons appearing in this book are not quoted verbatim but reproduced according to the sense and content.

ADRIAN LANGENSCHEID

TRUE CRIME CANADA

REAL CANADIAN CRIMINAL CASES

About this book:

Ice-cold serial killers, doomed family dramas, tragic kidnappings, vile torture, and ruthless abuse: thirteen shocking True Crime short stories based on true crime cases from Canada.

Captivated, stunned, amazed, and moved to tears, you will question everything you thought you knew about human nature. Life scripts horrifying stories and this book sums them up. Dive into the shocking world of true crime and real-life cases!

About the authors:

Adrian Langenscheid is the author of the successful True Crime International book series. His books have achieved bestseller status beyond the borders of Germany. Together with the podcasts "Mordgeflüster", "Überdosis Crime" and "Eyes in the Dark", the true crime expert continues the remarkable success of the predecessors with the ninth volume of the series.

Contents

History is not much more than an enumeration of the crimes, follies and misfortunes of mankind.

- Edward Gibbon (1737-1794)
British historian -

Preface

The last few years have held many surprises for me. Without great expectations and out of genuine interest, I have collected a wide variety of crime cases from many countries and published them in books. All of them have become bestsellers in the true crime genre. Now, with "True Crime Canada," you are holding the ninth book in the series in your hands.

The unexpected success and the public response humble me to this day. Partly because, looking back on my first two books, I would do a few things differently. I am very aware that this success would not have been possible without you, dear readers. That is why I dedicate this book to you. Thank you for your support, honest reviews and feedback. I read every single one.

Sincerely,

Your Adrian Langenscheid

Without reverence for life, humanity has no future.

- Albert Schweitzer (1875–1965)
French-German physician and philosopher-

CHAPTER 1

Release her from evil

The hands of his wristwatch are at twenty-five minutes past eleven on this October 24, 1993. Despite the wintry temperatures, the sky is bright blue, and the sun stands high on the horizon.

His wife Laura and the children would be back from the service in a few hours. It must be done by then. He must not lose any time. But had he thought things through carefully? If this actually worked, there would be no turning back. It would be over. Once and for all.

The longer the strong, broad-shouldered man with the round face, thick lips, blue eyes and brown-grey hair stares at the spiral-shaped suction tube in his massive hand, the more the certainty solidifies in him: he is doing the right thing. He can no longer just stand by and watch her suffer.

As if under the control of a stranger, he sticks one end of the hose deep into the exhaust pipe of his white and black 1982 GMC Sierra, which is parked in a garage near his house. He then climbs onto the back of the pickup and puts the other end of the hose through the sliding rear window into the interior of the car.

For almost two weeks he had racked his brain about how best to go about it. A drug overdose? A shot in the head? No. The arrangements would be too costly. In the end, he had opted for death by carbon monoxide intoxication. Easy, silent and, as far as anyone could tell, painless.

He jumps from the loading area and opens the driver's door. On the passenger seat is a mountain of old coats and a sleeping bag. The head of a child peeks out from underneath; a girl, it seems. She has wild, dark brown hair, a small snub nose and crooked teeth. The child looks at the man with glassy silver eyes, her open mouth forms into a smile.

The man gently strokes the child's head and presses a kiss to her forehead.

"Don't be afraid," he whispers to her. "Daddy is with you."

Mechanically, he pushes the clutch through with his foot, reaches for the ignition key and turns it to the right. The engine roars and the car shakes on its wheels. From now on, exhaust fumes incessantly pour into the interior of the pickup.

He gets out, throws the door shut from the outside and climbs onto the loading area again. There he settles down on an old tractor tire and watches the tangle through the rear window.

Will it take long for death to come? Will it be over after just a few seconds, or will it be miserably long minutes? In any case, one thing is certain: if she were to suffer unbearable agony and utter pleading sounds, he would stop it immediately.

But nothing happens. No sobs. No wistful cries. Had something possibly gone wrong? Had he made a mistake? Was there possibly a foreign body in the garden hose blocking the path of the exhaust gases? Or had the exact opposite happened, and the carbon monoxide had already done its work? But how was he supposed to check whether his plan was really working? Carbon monoxide is, after all, an invisible and at the same time odorless gas.

A glance at his watch. Twenty minutes to twelve. Three or four soft coughs can be heard from inside the car. Patience. He just has to hold out here a little longer.

Like the thousand-kilometer-long river of the Amazon rainforest, the labyrinth of fine, blood-red veins winds its way over white eyeballs. The swollen upper and lower eyelids have taken on a light pink color, tears trickle down the cheeks like little streams.

They are the marks of a long and nerve-wracking night on the faces of two new parents from Wilkie. The tranquil community of about 1300 people in the middle of the Canadian province of Saskatchewan is about an hour and a half's drive west of Saskatoon, the next largest city.

After settlers had moved to the previously uninhabited spot in 1905, Wilkie was officially incorporated as a town in 1910 and named after the former president of the Imperial Bank of Canada, Daniel Robert Wilkie. The names of the streets and avenues in the community also have something to do with the namesake or his bank.

Wilkie residents describe the community as a "friendly town" with tree-lined streets that meet both the medical and educational needs of all ages, as well as providing a safe and healthy family environment.

An environment situated between thousands and thousands of kilometers of meadows and pastures in the prairie province of Saskatchewan, which are mainly used for agricultural purposes. The numerous animals that live there - buffalo, bison or prairie dogs - all share a home alongside fields of corn and wheat.

On the outskirts of Wilkie lies the 520-hectare farm of the Latimer family, who have been cultivating rapeseed and grain for many decades, spanning generations.

It all started in 1948 when spouses Bill and May Latimer bought the farm and later moved in with their seven children. Three of the children came from May's first marriage; she had four more with her second husband Bill.

The second youngest child is Robert. An unassuming boy, born in 1953, he is known by those around him as always being spirited and kind and not hurting a fly. As he grows into a teenager, Robert discovers partying for himself. Not only does he make new contacts, but also gets into trouble with the law several times due to "impaired driving", i.e. driving under the influence of alcohol or drugs.

At the age of 21, the young adult is drawn to independence. He turned his back on Wilkie for the time being and left for British Columbia, where he pursued various professions. He even got his pilot's license. Three years later, in 1977, Robert decides it is time to return home.

No sooner has the 24-year-old settled back in Wilkie than he meets a pretty young woman with dark curly hair from British Columbia named Laura. She is in Wilkie for a short time to visit her grandparents. The two become close, fall in love and marry a year later. As Bill and May Latimer, Robert's parents, are about to retire at the time of their son's wedding, they leave the farm to the newlyweds and retire from the farming business. Two years later, life holds the next surprise for Robert and Laura: they are expecting their first child; a girl who is to be named Tracy.

When Laura goes into labor on the evening of November 22, 1980, the couple cannot know that their lives will change forever that night - in an unexpected way.

Robert drives his wife to a small hospital in the town of North Battleford on the North Saskatchewan River, about 60 kilometers away. It is only there that his wife notices that she had been bleeding unnaturally heavily in her private parts all along - a sign of a possible complication. To make matters worse, the heart rate monitor in her ward is broken, which is why the doctors initially don't know that the baby's heartbeat has slowed down.

When a working device can finally be found and they notice the girl's low heart rate, the doctors order Tracy to immediately be delivered by forceps. After the birth can be successfully carried out in this way, panic again spreads in the delivery room. New-born babies usually have their legs bent, but Tracy's tender little legs are stretched out and she is not breathing.

The medical staff manage to resuscitate the baby with cardiopulmonary massage and to stabilize her condition. Before Tracy undergoes further treatment, Robert and Laura are given a first, fleeting glimpse at their daughter.

The new parents look wistfully at the small, covered in vernix caseosa body. A nurse holds the child in her hands, fine, deep brown stubbles of hair sprouting on her head. Robert and Laura are overcome by a mixture of happiness and terrible sadness. Will Tracy manage to make a full recovery?

The next morning, the couple is told that the child has suffered several seizures and therefore has to be transferred to another hospital. The capacity of the small clinic in North Battleford is not sufficient to treat Tracy over a longer period of time. The girl is then taken to the Royal University Hospital in Saskatoon, about 135 kilometers away. There she is put into an artificial coma to reduce the swelling in her brain and minimize the risk of further seizures. It is not until five days after the birth that Laura is allowed to hold her first child in her arms for a few minutes.

Another three days later, Tracy is brought out of the coma. The seizures seem to have subsided, and the child is allowed home.

In March 1981, four months later, Robert notices that his daughter's hand has begun to twitch. Something he had already noticed in the hospital. Could the seizures be returning?

As a precaution, Robert and Laura immediately take Tracy back to the hospital. The child stays there for three months, during which the doctors carry out further examinations. They want to find out what exactly causes Tracy's seizures and how they can be treated.

Finally, a small ray of hope is provided by a mixture of different medicines that the doctors administer to the child in order to limit the seizures to five or six per day. But joy and sorrow lie close together in this case, too, as the doctors have meanwhile found out what causes Tracy's seizures: the lack of oxygen during birth has caused irreparable brain damage to the child. This brain damage eventually led to cerebral palsy; a term for the symptoms that can be traced back to the brain damage, such as movement disorders or muscle stiffness.

The diagnosis is the beginning of a stressful and painful existence for Tracy as the full extent of her condition gradually becomes apparent. The symptoms of cerebral palsy come in different forms and, depending on the individual, range from a simple movement disorder to severe spasticity. Tracy, on the other hand, has, according to the doctors, "the worst form of cerebral palsy" they have "ever seen". The girl has little to no voluntary control over the movements of her muscles, which means she can neither walk nor talk; only by using her eyes or laughing does she manage to communicate with those around her. With her limbs atrophied and her bones gradually shifting, Tracy is in constant pain.

Due to damage to her respiratory function as well as digestion, she often has difficulty breathing and eating; she often immediately vomits up the food she takes in. In addition, she is dependent on nappies and sits in a wheelchair from morning to night. According to the doctors, the girl has a maximum life expectancy of ten years and will be lucky if she reaches that age at all.

When Tracy is three years old, her brother Bryan is born. Despite Robert and Laura's worries that there could be complications with this birth, the boy is healthy. A year after his birth, Tracy has her first operation to relieve muscle tension in her left leg. But fatally, the operation has the exact opposite effect and leads to involuntary movements in Tracy's right leg and thus to further pain.

For Robert and Laura it is a great challenge to keep up the farm business on the one hand and to take care of their two children, especially the seriously ill Tracy, on the other. Despite the difficult situation and many shed tears, the couple never loses hope; always gives each other strength and learns to accept the special circumstances.

In 1985, little Lynsie is the third child born to the small Latimer family. Tracy is now five years old, at least physically. Mentally, the child is still at the level of an infant.

Despite her disability, Tracy finds enthusiasm in all the things other children her age do. She likes to listen to music, go swimming, watch the horses at the circus or watch TV. She has a very close bond with her family and loves it when her parents gently cradle her in their arms and spend time with her. Robert and Laura do everything in their power to give their daughter a carefree life, given the circumstances. They even send Tracy to a regular school and let her ride the school bus, which further encourages the child.

As she reaches the age of seven, Tracy has to vomit more and more frequently; her stomach can barely retain a meal, let alone her medication. She has increasing nutritional deficiencies and is rapidly losing weight, which is life-threatening in her situation.

The doctors order a feeding tube to be inserted into the child's stomach to supply her with the necessary amounts of food, fluids as well as her medicine. Robert and Laura, however, are skeptical about the procedure, as they believe it is the first step in keeping Tracy alive artificially. They do not want their daughter to be dependent on machines or other foreign bodies.

Robert and Laura's concern saves Tracy's life, as the doctors discover that the cause of her violent vomiting is the extremely high dose of anti-seizure medication, which has now become toxic to her. This is revealed when the amount of medication is reduced, and the problems seem to subside as a result. If Tracy had been force-fed her medicine, her stomach would have been destroyed.

Although this hurdle is overcome, fate continues to strike cruelly and does not let Tracy rest for a moment. Due to the severity of her cerebral palsy, other conditions develop, such as dislocation of the hip joints, or scoliosis, a three-dimensional deformation of the vertebrae that leads to an abnormal curvature of Tracy's back. By the time she is eight years old, her spine has already moved fifty degrees due to the scoliosis. As a result, the vital organs are under permanent pressure; the lungs and stomach are constricted. This makes it increasingly difficult for her to breathe, she suffers from chronic bronchitis, has to vomit even more frequently and has problems swallowing. In addition, she has repeated seizures.

In 1990, Tracy is about to turn ten, which is her predicted maximum life expectancy, she undergoes another operation. This time to lengthen her tendons and thus relieve the strain on her muscles. The operation goes well and Tracy seems to be slowly but surely on the road to recovery.

Two years later, however, Tracy's hip dislocation is getting worse; her spine has now shifted seventy degrees. In addition, her rib cage is pressing on her pelvis, causing Tracy excruciating pain and dramatically increasing the likelihood of her premature demise. For this reason, the doctors order another operation in which L-shaped stainless steel rods are implanted in her hip; wires hold them in place.

The successful operation means that Tracy's bones are no longer pressing on her vital organs, so she can breathe better and does not vomit as often. In addition, the child can now adopt a more comfortable sitting position. However, the operation also brings another setback - this time for Robert and Laura. Tracy has become stiff as a board because of the rods in her back, they complain. As a result, they can no longer cradle her in their arms in the same gentle way Tracy has always liked. Her sleeping position has also become more uncomfortable as a result. Laura explains that her daughter is no longer the happy and joyful young girl she was before her new operation.

In February 1993, the girl is now twelve years old, still has the cognitive abilities of a new-born and her hip is once again dislocated. The doctors, however, do not want to perform surgery right away as they feel Tracy needs a little more recovery time from her last operation.

As Laura becomes pregnant for the fourth time, her belly grows with the fear that she will no longer be able to care for Tracy and withstand the psychological pressure that comes with it. After long and careful consideration, Robert and Laura come to the joint conclusion that it is best to place Tracy in a home in North Battleford at the end of the pregnancy.

Just two months after the birth of little Lee, the Latimers bring their daughter home to them. Although Tracy did well in the home, she lost a lot of weight in the meantime because the carers were not familiar with the method of feeding the child properly.

As soon as they have the girl back with them, Laura takes her daughter to Dr. Dzus, an orthopaedic surgeon, to discuss the next steps of treatment for Tracy. The family is desperate and exhausted; farm life and caring for four children, one of whom is in need of care, are wearing on their nerves.

As the doctor enters the treatment room, she instantly realises how much pain Tracy must actually be in. "Her mother held her right leg in the air in a bent position and every time you tried to move the leg, Tracy would express pain and cry out," Dzus recalls.

Tracy's right hip bone has been badly affected over the years, causing the girl great anguish. However, reconstruction of the hip is not feasible because of the massive damage to the spherical joint. One could try to remove her femur, Dzus muses, leaving the leg connected to Tracy's body only by muscles and tendons. The recovery time for this operation would be about a year and would cause pain in her joints. Suffering that can only be alleviated by further operations - a never-ending cycle.

The post-operative pain would be so intense that the only short-term solution would be an epidural, i.e., medication to anaesthetise the spinal nerves. The problem is that the painkillers, in combination with the medication for her seizures, would cause Tracy to have new seizures, stomach bleeding, constipation, aspiration and aspiration pneumonia, i.e., the aspiration of saliva and the resulting pneumonia.

Back home, Laura tearfully informs her husband that the date for the all-important operation is set for three weeks from now, on November 4, 1993.

The lights are switched off and the curtains drawn when Laura enters her daughter's room at around 1:30 pm on October 24, 1993. She had just returned from church service with the rest of the family and had immediately prepared lunch upon her arrival.

But one place at the dining table remains empty: Tracy's. The girl had stayed at home with her father Robert and, according to him, was taking a nap. Laura then sets out to wake her daughter.

As the caring mother approaches the bed, she immediately notices that something is wrong. The skin on Tracy's round face is strangely pale. Panicking, Laura calls for her husband; he should call an ambulance immediately. She grabs Tracy under the arms and pulls her upper body upwards, her legs dangling limply in the air. At that moment Laura realises: her daughter is dead.

Despite the dismay and the pain of her soul, Laura also feels a kind of peace inside her. Peace for her daughter, who now no longer has to suffer.

At 2 p.m. that same day, the Royal Canadian Mounted Police (RCMP) receive an emergency call. Robert Latimer answers the phone. The sturdy farmer explains that his daughter Tracy has died unexpectedly in her sleep.

A short time later, several police officers accompanied by a coroner appear on the farm's doorstep. While the latter examines Tracy's body, Robert tells the officers in great detail what is supposed to have happened. He had put Tracy in her bed at around 12:30 a.m. because she was once again in tremendous pain. When Laura wanted to wake up their daughter for lunch, she noticed that Tracy had died in her sleep.

Unable to determine the exact cause of death at first glance, the coroner orders an autopsy on Tracy. For some reason, however, Robert seems to object. He would prefer Tracy to be cremated and put in the ground as soon as possible, he announces.

As this sentence leaves Robert's lips, his wife looks at him in wonder. They exchange a few glances and then disappear together into the bedroom. What exactly they talk about is not known, but when the two return a few minutes later, Laura is also convinced that Tracy should be cremated. The police are sceptical: did Tracy truly die in her sleep? Or is Robert hiding something? Is the girl's death possibly a mercy killing, a deliberate killing to end her suffering?

Against Robert's and Laura's protests, the autopsy is carried out a day later in Saskatoon by Dr. Ranjit Waghray. Although the pathologist cannot initially determine an unusual cause of death, he discovers a high concentration of carbon monoxide in Tracy's blood. A sign of possible poisoning? Waghray orders a blood test.

Tracy's body is buried among the closest family members on October 27, 1993. A few days later, Dr Waghray receives the results of the blood test, which leave no doubt: Tracy's blood contains a carbon monoxide level of 80 percent - a value that suggests that the girl was deliberately exposed to the gas. But by whom? Her father? Robert had been the only one to stay home with his daughter on that October 24, 1993, while the rest of the family was at church. Is that why he had reacted so nervously when the coroner ordered an autopsy? Did he want to prevent traces of murder from being found in a possible inquest?

On the morning of November 4, 1993, the day Tracy's operation was supposed to take place, Sergeant Bob Conlon and Corporal Ken Lyons are standing on the doorstep of Latimer Farm. When Robert opens the door, they tell him that he is the prime suspect in his daughter's murder. They ask him to get dressed and come with them; to the North Battleford police station where he would be asked some questions about this. While Robert gets dressed and accompanies the officers outside, his wife Laura remains visibly confused and alone back in Wilkie with the children.

Corporal Lyons knows who he is dealing with and doesn't beat around the bush. As soon as Robert sits in front of him in the small interrogation cell, he confronts him directly with the accusations.

"From what we know about you and your family, I have no doubt that you killed your daughter," Lyons says in a calm voice. "I know you loved Tracy and I also know that you didn't really want to do this."

Robert's eyes fill with tears and his head tilts forward almost imperceptibly.

"But you had to do it," Lyons continues. "For her. Am I right?"

Robert doesn't answer.

"We know you are a hard-working and loving father," Lyons says. "And we also know that you did it out of love for your daughter."

Again, Robert does not comment on the allegations. Only when Corporal Lyons asks him the question over and over again does the farmer break his silence.

"I wanted to put her out of her misery," he says in a brittle voice. Tears now run in rivulets down his face.

"Considering you don't have a lawyer," Lyons says after a while, "I advise you that this confession could get you charged with murder."

Robert nods. "I know," he says.

Lyons takes a deep breath. "Then please tell us what happened on that October 24," he says, taking out a piece of paper and pen in the absence of a recording device and listening to the family father's story.

After Laura took Tracy to see Doctor Dzus on October 12, 1993, and he, Robert, was informed of the plan to operate on Tracy again, he made the decision that it was time to finally put an end to her torment.

He said he spent the next two weeks mostly wondering "how?". Should he poison Tracy with an overdose of Valium? Shoot her in the head? No. In the end, he had opted for death by carbon monoxide poisoning.

Why he chose October 24, 1993, exactly, Robert doesn't know. After Laura and the children had left for the service at around eleven o'clock, he had simply seized the opportunity.

As soon as his family was out of the house, Robert went to the tin shed and took out a spiral suction hose for water tanks. He put it in the back of his pickup and drove to his workshop on the farm, where he got some old rags, two large boxes and a hacksaw. He also threw these utensils into the back of the truck and drove to his garage where he parked the truck.

Robert then went to the apartment building to get his daughter. He took Tracy to the garage, lifted her out of her wheelchair and put her in the passenger seat of the pickup. Robert stuffed the rags between Tracy's back and the cushion to allow her to sit upright. Then he covered her body with two old coats as well as a sleeping bag; he left her face exposed.

Robert got out and took the hacksaw with which he cut the suction hose. Plastic shavings trickled onto the garage floor. He stuck one end of the shortened hose deep into the exhaust pipe and put the other end through the sliding rear window into the interior. At 11:30 a.m. he turned on the engine, sat on an old tractor tyre in the back of the pickup and watched his daughter die. If Tracy suffered excruciating pain, he would call it off immediately.

Half an hour later, around noon, it had been done. Tracy was dead.

Robert jumped off the truck bed with shaky knees, opened the driver's door and switched off the engine. Then he took the hose out of the exhaust and threw it back onto the loading area.

He took his daughter's lifeless body, put it in the wheelchair and took Tracy to her room. There he laid her in her bed to make it appear that she had died in her sleep; Robert burned the evidence of his murder.

Corporal Lyons wants to know whether Laura had been informed about the plans to kill Tracy, whereupon Robert explains that he had informed his wife of his intentions on the evening of October 12, 1993, i.e., directly after the doctor's visit. However, he also emphasises that his wife had never been involved in the planning of the crime and had merely shared her "general" thoughts about it with him. For example, she had considered consulting Dr Jack Kevorkian, a pathologist who helps people commit suicide. These thoughts, however, had been purely theoretical, if Tracy's killing were to be considered as a last resort.

If Laura was supposed to have been informed of her husband's plans, why did she not prevent the act? She left Robert alone with Tracy on that October 24,1993, knowing full well that he intended to murder her. Did she not trust him to actually carry out the deed? Or did she deliberately not stop her husband from his plans? Is Laura indirectly involved in the murder after all?

Robert spends a total of four days in prison before he is released on bail. However, his freedom is given to him under some restrictions; he is only allowed to leave the province of Saskatchewan with permission, has to report to the police every Friday and is not allowed to drink a single drop of alcohol.

In the meantime, national as well as international media have caught wind of the family man's crime. This draws unwanted attention to the Latimers; heated discussions are held about Robert's moral motives. If for some he is a selfless hero who acted solely out of love for his daughter, others say he is a cold-blooded murderer who snuffed out the life of a child who did not even know how to defend herself.

The case quickly becomes one of the most controversial murder cases in Canadian criminal history. Above all, the question of whether Robert gave his daughter the coup de grace is at the forefront.

From a purely legal point of view, however, the matter seems to be quickly settled. In the 1990s, euthanasia was generally not legal in Canada; moreover, it could only be carried out by doctors, if at all. In Tracy's case, however, this does not play a major role anyway, because the dying person must consent to his or her death. Tracy, with her twelve years of life and her cognitive abilities of a new-born, was neither able to consent to her death nor to express a concrete wish to die. Was Robert acting solely in his own interest?

On November 7, 1994, 41-year-old Robert Latimer is on trial for first-degree murder, i.e., premeditated killing. The judges and jurors face a daunting task: despite the moral and ethical debate, they must deliver a just verdict and not let their own emotions get the better of them.

Laura, who was originally supposed to appear as the last witness for the prosecution, changes sides shortly before the trial begins and now appears as the last witness for the defence. Her statement reads:

"Tracy's birth was a lot sadder than her death. We lost our daughter when she was born."

Laura also reports on the relationship between Robert and Tracy: "He was a wonderful and loving father. He was always there for Tracy, loved her very much and she loved him."

The Crown Prosecutor, on the other hand, claims the exact opposite about Robert. He killed his daughter, he says, solely to lift the burden from him and his wife. For this claim, he gets a warning from the judge.

After about four hours of deliberation by the jury, Robert Latimer is found guilty not of first-degree murder but of second-degree murder, i.e., manslaughter. Earlier, the judge had told the jury that if they found Robert guilty, they would have the choice of convicting him of first or second degree murder. Many see the judge's statement as a kind of invitation to find the defendant guilty; accordingly, the jurors would have had no other choice.

However, because Robert admitted to the crime, the jurors really had no choice but to find him guilty. If they had not done so, they would have disregarded the law. In exceptional cases, however, the jury also has the right to disregard evidence as well as the law if they deem it unfair, unjust or immoral in any way - so-called "jury nullification". Since the defence is prohibited from advising the jurors of this right, and the prosecution had no reason to do so in Robert's case, nullification was waived.

Before the sentence is pronounced, Robert is given the last word. He says he remains convinced that he did the right thing. If it is not a crime to cut off Tracy's leg, implant a feeding tube or let her live with this pain for another twenty years, it should not be a crime to put her out of her misery.

The verdict is reached: Robert Latimer is sentenced to ten years imprisonment without parole.

After the trial, Laura criticises the Canadian legal system to the assembled press, saying that a wonderful and loving father should not simply be locked away. Robert could not, under any circumstances, relate in prison to what Tracy had endured for almost thirteen years.

A week later, Robert appeals against the verdict, which is rejected by the Court of Appeal of Canada on July 18, 1995, by a vote of 2:1. The verdict thus stands for the time being, until there is a surprising twist three months later:

It is revealed that the Crown prosecutor apparently questioned possible jurors on the subjects of religion, abortion as well as mercy killing before the first trial. As the Supreme Court considers this to be jury interference, it orders another trial against Robert Latimer in February 1997. The trial begins on October 27, 1997, three days after Tracy's fourth death anniversary. Robert's confession remains valid; he is now charged with second-degree murder.

The second trial is almost identical to the first. Laura, who takes the stand again, explains to the defence that she was initially "angry and shocked" when she heard her husband admit to the crime. However, she was also happy to find Tracy's lifeless body. Laura was not mourning the death of her daughter, but her birth.

The court wants to know if she had known that Tracy could be killed by Robert. Laura answers with a clear "no"; when she went to church with the rest of the family on that October 24, 1993, she had not known that Robert was planning a murder. She thought Tracy had died of a seizure in her sleep.

Laura explains why she jumped to this conclusion, when Tracy and her room should have smelled of car exhaust, by saying that Robert was a "one hundred percent honest man" and that she therefore had no reason to mistrust him.

In the further course of the trial, Laura's diary entries are also analysed. In them, she describes Tracy as a happy child who liked to get up to mischief. Six days before her death, she even ate well. In court, however, Laura now claims that her daughter had been subjected to constant suffering and had been in terrible pain from morning to night. Confronted with this accusation, Laura explains that she had pounced on every last bit of her daughter's happiness. The diary entries are thus not meant to be a general picture of Tracy's life, but rather to depict her few happy moments.

After a week of questioning several witnesses, examining Tracy's circumstances from all sides and describing Robert over and over again as a loving and caring father, the jury finds the farmer guilty of second-degree murder.

When the verdict is pronounced, Laura jumps up from her seat and loudly voices her indignation. Again and again, the word "no" echoes off the courtroom walls.

Robert turns to her and tries to calm her down. "It's okay," he says. "It's okay."

The minimum sentence for second-degree murder calls for a prison term of at least ten years, but the jury recommends that the court release Robert on parole after one year in prison.

The judge takes note of this advice and sentences Robert Latimer to a prison term of two years, of which he is to serve one year each in prison and one year at home under close supervision. He justifies this on the grounds that Robert was driven to commit the offence by compassion towards his daughter and thus one would make a constitutional exception to disregard the prescribed ten years' imprisonment.

The Crown Prosecution Service appeals this decision, arguing that Robert should serve the ten-year minimum sentence for his crime. The Saskatchewan Court of Appeal agrees with the Crown Prosecution Service and sentences Robert to life imprisonment.

Robert is now appealing this sentence to the Supreme Court as he feels he has been treated unfairly. He was denied the opportunity to explain his motives for the murder in detail; he still believes that he had no choice but to end his daughter's life with his own hands. Accordingly, a life sentence was too cruel and unusual in his eyes.

The Supreme Court does not enter into any discussion and unanimously decides that the sentence will stand. Thus, it becomes final and Robert's life sentence remains, which he begins on January 18, 2001, at William Head Institution, thirty kilometres west of Victoria in British Columbia. Almost ten years later, in December 2010, his prison sentence is suspended; Robert is allowed to leave prison.

Laura supported her husband throughout the trial and did not leave his side even when thick reinforced concrete facades came between them. The Latimers are happily married to this day.

Robert's view of things has not changed either. He did, in his view, the only right thing and would do it again if circumstances demanded it. Asked if he knew whether Tracy wanted to die or not, the family man replies:

"I assume that she did not want to suffer any more pain. I can only go by what I would have wanted for myself."

Humans do not know which place to occupy, they have obviously made a mistake and have descended from their true place without being able to find it again. Restless and without success, they search for it everywhere in its inscrutable darkness.

- Blaise Pascal (1623-1662) French mathematician, physicist, man of letters and Christian philosopher -

CHAPTER 2

You cannot stop it!

Ryan Boyle hastily scrolls through the entire page of suggestions on YouTube. The announced video must be somewhere! The ex-soldier, who is active on the Internet under the name "Save Kitty", wants to check what really lies behind this disturbing clip, which is repeatedly referred to in the forums. Hot discussions are going on whether it is a true act or a bad joke. The disturbing clues have attracted active animal rights activist to the video clip platform on this day, December 21, 2010. What is behind the strange title "1 guy - 2 kittens"? The man stares at the screen and tensely skims title after title of the videos that other users have uploaded. Stop! Indeed, there it is!

Trembling with agitation, he clicks on the video clip with the kittens on the thumbnail. Deep down in his mind, there's still a tiny spark of hope that it's all just a bad joke, a fake to push the video's reach. But in the very first seconds, the passionate animal rights activist realizes: this is cruel reality! A man, whose face cannot be seen, grabs two small baby cats and then puts them into a ready plastic bag. Next, the man picks up the waiting vacuum cleaner and puts the tube into the plastic bag; after it is sealed, he turns on the vacuum cleaner. Within a fraction of a second, the man thus sucks all the breathing air out of the bag and finally, after a gruesome death struggle, the two innocent kittens suffocate.

It takes Boyle half a moment to regain his composure, but then he takes action and creates a Facebook group titled "Find the Vacuum Kitten Killer for Great Justice." His goal is clear: The unknown person must be found and held accountable before something like this happens again! Within a very short time, the group grows to around 4,000 members, all of whom have the same goal as Boyle, to bring the animal abuser to justice and prevent further, similar acts by potential copycats. To this end, the most urgent goal of the group is to find out the name and address of the unknown person.

Quickly the assumption arises that the animal abuser could be one of the group members - but under a different name or even with several accounts. Certain entries and behaviors strongly suggest that the man has sneaked in. Does he want to gloat over his dubious fame? Especially when, sometime later, pictures from the video with the two kittens are posted by exactly these users - but presumably from a different version of the video. For on the images the face of the perpetrator can be clearly seen this time. On December 28, 2010, the animal rights activists offer a reward. The person who can provide clues that lead to the capture of the Vacuum Kitten Killer will receive 5,000 dollars (about 4400 GBP). Joe Panz, an acquaintance of Boyle who is one of the founding members of the Facebook group, warns, "Animal cruelty is a gateway crime." He is certain, "If someone goes through that door, even much worse things will happen!"

The activists' research ultimately focuses on the Facebook account of a young Canadian man named Luka Magnotta, who shared yet another gruesome video on his Facebook page earlier this fall. The title of the clip is "3 guys 1 hammer". The content is diabolical, but is the man actually identical to the cat killer? The video shows how a man is brutally attacked by three perpetrators with a hammer and finally even beaten to death with it. Even though the account owner was apparently not involved in this barbaric act himself (he cannot be seen in the video), the distribution of the clip nevertheless allows an insight into the mental attitude of the uploader. One of the comments under the clip says: "Luka is not able to live if there is no chaos in his existence. Only then does it feel like he matters." Animal lovers are wondering if this might be another fake account made by Magnotta. Who else could know something so personal about him? Furthermore, they witness the man boasting several times that he is the current boyfriend of the infamous Karla Homolka, a very well-known Canadian serial killer. However, he later admits that he only made up the relationship with the woman. The 28-year-old is doing it to get attention. He is so obsessed with being the center of attention and a celebrity that he even had a heated dispute with Wikipedia, the largest Internet encyclopedia, in 2008. On two occasions, the opponents even meet in court, because Magnotta does not shy away from an expensive lawsuit in order to enforce his supposed rights. The man pulls out all the stops to immortalize himself with an entry about himself on the Internet - but the online encyclopedia consistently opposes this and is also proven right in court.

At the beginning of 2011, a new Facebook group was founded, the Animal Beta Project or AB Project, a successor group to the one Boyle had set up. The eleven members are determined to do everything necessary to stop the animal abuser from committing further acts. This time, they even go so far as to analyze every single image of the cat murder clip in detail and compare it with the photos that their main suspect posts online. The matches of furnishings and clothing are striking! The next step is to scrutinize the images even more closely to track the person in real life - another bull's eye. The cat killer posted the photos along with the exact shooting data recorded by the cell phone camera. With this, the animal rights activists were even able to locate the place where the man is currently staying Toronto. Immediately, the animal welfare organization Ontario Society for the Prevention of Cruelty to Animals is contacted. The members pass the information received directly to the local police department. The news that the officers are finally investigating the case is like salvation for the animal lovers. Done!" they rejoice. -But at the end of 2011, the animal tormentor once again posts disturbing videos of his deeds online.

This time, a kitten is fed to a python by a man wearing a Christmas hat, but whose face cannot be seen. In a second clip, a man ties a young kitten to a broomstick with duct tape and drowns the completely defenceless animal in the bathtub.

Now even the British tabloid "The Sun" reports about the kitten killer. One day, the suspect shows up in the London editorial office completely unexpectedly. The young man claims that he has nothing whatsoever to do with all the animal cruelty. Two days after this visit, which is described by the editors as extremely strange, the editor who spoke to him receives an e-mail with alarming content. The message sends shivers down the spines of even the most hardened tabloid journalists: "The next time you hear from me it will be about a movie I'm producing - but then it will have some people in it, not just kittens." It goes on to say, "Killing is not like smoking a cigarette. Once you taste blood, you can't stop. You can't stop it! And to get away with it is just brilliant." Despite this disturbing announcement, the matter is not being pursued. Although the journalists forward the email to the authorities and report the uncanny encounter with Luka Magnotta, the London police do not feel responsible for it, since the acts did not happen in the UK and, moreover, there is no extradition request from Canada. Only the animal rights activists continue to keep their suspect in their sights. They are sure that he now lives in Montreal, since the environment in his photos has changed and now clearly depicts the largest city in the Canadian province of Quebec. What no one suspects is that Luka Magnotta is now mainly involved on the Internet with sites that are either about necrophilia (sexual preference directed at corpses) or tranquilizers. Kittens are now no longer of interest to him.

Cat lover Ryan Boyle, in particular, continues to keep a watchful eye on the VKK. As a result, he is one of the first to discover the Facebook postings on May 15 and 16, 2012. For two days, hints of a video were posted over and over again, though it's not even online at this point. But at least a photo from it is posted online, showing a man in a purple hoodie - holding an ice pick in his raised right hand. The title of the clip doesn't bode well either, with its echoes of the perpetrator's previous violent videos. Above the video's thumbnail are the words "1 Lunatic 1 Ice Pick" in thick letters. In a post in the comment columns on Facebook, people explicitly ask where they can find the video. Boyle automatically gives the impression that this is the cat killer's usual approach. Announcing something in advance and then using other alias accounts to further push the interest of users.

The next few days the comment section will be a little quieter about the video with the strange, alarming title. On May 24, 2012, however, it suddenly goes completely silent. The man, who is still the VKK for animal rights activists, suddenly disappears from the face of the earth. As if a black hole had opened up and devoured him whole. Not a single comment or post is uploaded by the VKK anymore.

On the same day, Jun Lin, an enrolled Chinese student studying engineering and computer science at Montreal's Concordia University, fails to show up at his part-time job as a clerk at a supermarket.

Only one day later, on Friday, the announced video "1 Lunatic 1 Ice Pick" actually appears on the Internet. This time, however, it is not uploaded to YouTube, but can be found on the ominous website bestgore.com. The site owner, Czech Mark Marek, has made it his goal to show users the brutality in this world completely unfiltered. The operator allows videos to be uploaded ranging from documented suicides to atrocities that take place in war zones. And even with regard to the brutal video with the ice pick, he apparently has no qualms about leaving the scenes on his portal.

In the first shots, a young man can be seen lying on a bed - handcuffed to the bed frame. In the next shot, the handcuffed man on the bed seems strangely lifeless, as if he were stunned - or even dead? Suddenly, another figure appears and abruptly brutally attacks the body. With a screwdriver that has been converted into an ice pick, the attacker stabs the bound man again and again. It almost seems as if the ice pick murder from the movie "Basic Instinct" is to be re-enacted. At some point, the perpetrator lets go of his victim, but only to reach for a knife and a fork. He then begins to cut pieces out of the bound man. The dog present is also encouraged to chew on one of the corpse's legs. After this, the desecrated corpse is cut up with a serrated knife. Finally, the killer performs anal sex with the torso of the victim. The video lasts almost eleven agonizingly long minutes. Only then do the gruesome images, which are accompanied by the soundtrack of the cult film "American Psycho," end.

Although Roger Renville, a civil litigation lawyer living in Montana, USA, informed the Toronto police over the weekend about the video he came across on Saturday morning, they paid no attention to his tip. The lawyer even emphasizes that he believes the video shows the murder and subsequent dismemberment of a real person. The Toronto police simply say that the lawyer's story does not make sense. And the lawyer is countered with the question: "Why would a killer film himself and then put that on the Internet?" The law enforcement officers leave it at that. They do not even view the clip in question pro forma. To this day, however, the police deny that they simply ignored the tip.

The full extent of the terrible crime comes to light only in the following days. On Tuesday, May 29, 2012, a strange mail package arrives at the Conservative Party headquarters in Ottawa; addressed to incumbent Prime Minister Stephen Harper. The package is directly noticed in the mailroom of number 130 on Albert Street by a strange, unpleasantly sweet smell. The suspicion quickly arises that the brown stains could be blood. However, no one is prepared for what is inside the package sent by Canada Post. The police arrive at 11:20 a.m. and immediately classify the possibly bloodstained package as dangerous goods and call in the appropriate department. They finally open the package carefully so as not to destroy any traces and are confronted with a discovery that is a real shock even for these experts: Inside the package is a severed, decomposing human foot.

Another package is addressed to Liberal headquarters, but it is already sorted out at the Canada Post parcel sorting office because of its strange appearance and smell and is opened there. Inside this package is a severed hand. Nobody suspects at this point that the body parts could have something to do with the video "1 Lunatic 1 Ice-pick".

Immediately, questions arise for the investigators: Are these mysterious parcels possibly the message of a mentally ill person or an assassin? Furthermore, the police immediately contacted all the mortuaries and funeral homes. They want to find out whether body parts have been stolen somewhere in the last few days. But the most important and at the same time worst find is still to come.

On this Tuesday morning, another sensational discovery is made in the district in Montreal's Côte-des-Neiges neighborhood. Janitor Mike Nadeau is out on a morning patrol at about 10:15. He is in charge of a residential building on the corner of Place

Lucy and Décarie, west of Décarie Boulevard. Several residents have complained to him about a terrible stench coming from the large pile of garbage behind the house. Such complaints are nothing new for the experienced janitor. Presumably, someone has been wildly disposing of their trash here once again. And now he has to deal with it. The janitor quickly identifies the source of the really bad smell at the garbage heap: The stench is coming from an old, carelessly discarded suitcase. Nadeau had already noticed it last Friday. But on this Tuesday, a strange transformation happened to it. White maggots crawl and squirm all over the suitcase. The janitor is getting restless. He calls in one of his employees to open the suitcase together.

Mike's gut feeling does not deceive him. As the lid flips open, a view of something bloated and remotely reminiscent of something human is revealed. But what should be rosy skin is strangely greenish and waxy, downright marbled. And covering it all, an almost unbearable, sickeningly sweet stench! "We're out of here, call the police!" he's still yelling, and steps back in horror. For in the suitcase is a gradually decomposing human torso - without a head.

Now, finally, the police investigation begins. Although the investigation is initially open-ended, it is quickly suspected that the human body parts in Ottawa and Montreal are the remains of a single person. Soon, the man seen in the videos is also given a name. Montreal police discover the same male person on May 29, 2012, both on surveillance camera footage from a Canada Post outlet and on footage from a video camera mounted on the building in Côte-des-Neiges. The assumption is obvious that the unknown person is the wanted man.

One day later, on May 30, 2012, the police view the video "1 Lunatic 1 Ice-Pick" for the very first time. While analyzing the murder video, the officers receive another decisive tip from the operator of the website bestgore.com: Marek gives the TV station

CBC News the decisive tip that visitors to his website have identified the person responsible for the video. It was a young man named Luka Rocco Magnotta - also known as Eric Clinton Newman and under the pseudonym Vladimir Romanov. And suddenly also the animal-cruelly kitten videos are again of relevance, with which the name Magnotta was brought in connection by numerous Internet users again and again.

On the same day, Magnotta's apartment is finally searched by the police. Several other tenants in the building have already complained to the landlord about the stench emanating from the young man's apartment into the hallway. The smell is reminiscent of rotten meat. Eric Schorer, the building manager, is present and is questioned in detail before the police officers enter the apartment. According to him, Magnotta has only been living here for four months. However, no one has seen the young man for some time. Magnotta had been a pleasant, uncomplicated tenant; he had passed the required credit check without any problems. Apart from that, he never gave any cause for complaint, for example because of noise.

The truth about the tenant with the blue eyes and dark hair, who is described as about 1.78 meters tall and weighing around 65 kilos, becomes apparent the moment the police officers enter the abandoned apartment. The stench that hits the investigators is indescribable. It even penetrates the police officers' breathing masks and causes a nauseating feeling in the stomach area. What shocking images: blood is everywhere, on the walls, on the floor.

While one part of the investigation team takes a closer look at the apartment, other colleagues start questioning the neighbors. The police present the tenants with two photos: one of Magnotta and one of the possible victim, the student Jun Lin. The two could be identified together on footage from the building's surveillance camera, just as they are about to enter the building together. Luka

Rocco Magnotta the interviewees recognize immediately, but they have doubts about the other picture. In any case, this man cannot have been here often, otherwise they would certainly have noticed him.

When examining the pile of garbage behind the building where Magnotta's apartment is located, a screwdriver turned into an ice pick, a hammer, a knife and saws are discovered - with traces of blood on them. Among all the garbage, the police officers also come across the carcass of a dog. The dead animal is lying next to blood-stained clothes and a bloody shower curtain.

Regarding the person Magnotta, the Montreal police is rather taciturn and seems uninformed: They say he is otherwise a blank slate and not known to the police - neither in Montreal nor elsewhere. Calculation or bad research? The journalists from CBC News obviously have better sources or dig deeper. They quickly find out that Magnotta was not only convicted of fraud four times in Ontario in 2005. He was actually in prison - 16 days in pre-trial detention, 9 months suspended prison sentence. On top of that, 12 months of probation as well. So, actually a blank slate?

Luka Rocco Magnotta, was born as Eric Clinton Kirk Newman on July 24, 1982, in Scarborough, Ontario. He is born into problematic family circumstances; both parents are minors. His father Donald Newman is an alcoholic and suffers from schizophrenia. His mother, Anna Yourkin, just 16, is also mentally unstable and struggles with obsessive-compulsive disorder. She often wears a medical face mask and rubber gloves. She is scrupulous about cleanliness, which is why she herself constantly washes her three children's hands. Eric is the youngest of the Yorkin's children and is home-schooled by his mother Anna for the first few years. Only after he is old enough for the sixth grade does he attend the local elementary school for some time. Little Eric grows up in this family climate. He even has to witness how his mother finally puts his rabbits outside the door in winter so that they freeze to death. Furthermore, she repeatedly locks the children in the house or in the car. At least this is what Magnotta later claims. Fact: His parents separate early: when Eric's father is committed to a psychiatric institution in 1994 and files for divorce, the boy is 12 years old.

His overwhelmed mother, herself mentally ill, gives the boy to his grandmother Phyllis and grandfather, with whom he is supposed to live from now on. Phyllis has very rigid views about the world outside. She is firmly convinced that the earth is a dirty and dangerous place. Eric is therefore taken out of mainstream school for a while after two years by Phyllis Yourkin and taught at home. However, Grandma Phyllis' world is also anything but perfect. She separates from her husband; the couple's divorce follows. Eric's grandmother seeks comfort from her grandson in a strange way, at least that's how he reports it later. Eric says that Phyllis slept in the same bed with him. Rumor has it that the grandmother was even abusive. Phyllis often dressed her grandson in her own clothes, so that the little boy looked like a girl at first sight. If the homophobic Phyllis caught Eric playing with Barbie dolls, however, he was called a "faggot" in the worst possible way, and his brother Conrad and sister Melissa did the same. A cousin not only made fun of Eric's acne, which blossomed during puberty, and hurt the boy's soul with it; he is also said to have sexually abused him several times when he was 14 years old. At least, that's the recollection of Eric Clinton Kirk Newman. Classmates and teachers who met him between 1998 and 2000 describe Newman as extremely vain. He was constantly preoccupied with his appearance.

In 1999, Eric is 17 years old. That year, he visits a psychiatrist for the first time after telling his grandmother that he is hearing voices. The teenager also speaks loudly and repeatedly suffers from anxiety. After a psychiatrist diagnoses him with paranoid schizophrenia, Eric drops out of high school. The teenager is granted severely disabled status and is given a place in a psychiatric residential group. Here, he repeatedly mentions to the other roommates that he feels persecuted by the government and that his phone is bugged. Eric's aunt later tells a newspaper, "He's sick in the head and a megalomaniac."

In 2002, Eric Newman is now 20 years old, he takes his first job. He starts stripping in a nightclub. A short time later, he also appears as a performer in porn films. The young man is even active as a male escort, under the pseudonym "Jimmy". Two years later, Newman tries to find a new source of money: he befriends a 21-year-old woman who is on the mental level of a child of about 10 years. He has her apply for a credit card and maxes it out to the last cent. Newman manages to squander just under 10,000 dollars (about 8800 GBP) until the bank cuts him off. The police pursue the credit card fraud and in the course of the investigation, more details quickly come to light. The initial allegation that Newman had also sexually assaulted the 21-year-old and videotaped his crime, however, is dropped in the course of the trial. According to his own attorney, Peter Scully, a fatal decision that changed Newman's life "immeasurably, with enormous implications for our society." At this point, no one suspects just how right he is to be. At the very least, he is convicted of fraud. At the sentencing, the judge in charge, Lauren Marshall, once again strongly admonishes Newman: "You have a medical problem and must always take medication." But the judge's stern words won't make the defendant change his ways.

After his conviction, Newman continues to work as a porn performer. He also poses for homosexual men's magazines. Occasionally, he wears women's clothing. In early 2006, he meets transgender woman Barbie and tells his new acquaintance, who was born male but identifies as a woman, that he will definitely be a big celebrity one day. Barbie constantly has to take photos of Newman, which he uses to decorate the personal cult shrine in his apartment. In the summer of 2006, Newman finally adopts a new, more sonorous name, which he believes is more befitting of a celebrity. He officially renames himself Luka Rocco Magnotta.

Following a private bankruptcy, Magnotta now at last wants to land in showbiz. In 2007 and 2008, he auditions for several reality show formats, including "Cover Guy," a six-part Canadian program in which thirty young men do everything they can to make it as a male model. One of the prizes is being featured on Canada's "abOUT" magazine. Justifying why he, of all people, would be the ideal model for a cover photo, Magnotta tells the stunned judges with a chest-pounding conviction, "Some people say I'm devastatingly good-looking." At this point, Magnotta's gait has also changed; he now constantly moves as if he were a model presenting the latest haute couture on a catwalk. At least, that's how the 70-year-old man describes it, whom Magnotta allowed to accompany him on several trips overseas in 2009. In the various photos from metropolises such as Paris, New York, Moscow and Rome that appear on social networks, Magnotta can often be seen in provocative poses - bare-chested; lips made up in garish pink or red. By this time, he has already undergone several plastic surgeries.

In December 2010, his journey in search of public fame comes to an end; Magnotta has tried almost all the options open to him to become a star - without success. Yet he has always been so fascinated by female movie stars like Marilyn Monroe, Ava Gardner and Sharon Stone, the murdering star of the classic film Basic Instinct. But now he finally knows how to get everyone's attention - with a bang! To do so, he gets himself an innocent kitten ...

While the police are still searching for Magnotta, he has long since disappeared. His trail disappears on May 26, 2012, at a Canadian airport, where the young man boards a plane bound for France. A worldwide dragnet search is initiated in cooperation with Interpol. For this purpose, the data of persons in question are stored during police checks at state borders and compared with the data of the target person by the public prosecutor's office. This form of tracing may only be used if no other options are available and a judge or public prosecutor orders dragnet searches. This type of tracing is only used at all for certain, serious criminal offenses. Everything humanly possible is done to track down the murderer as quickly as possible. After all, at the time of his visit to the London newspaper "The Sun", he had already indicated to a reporter that he could not let go of this ultimate kick. Urgency is the order of the day!

In Montreal, investigators have now made important progress: Magnotta's dismembered and violated victim has been identified by DNA test! It concerns the Chinese student Jun Lin. The self-confessed homosexual 33-year-old, who is called Justin by his friends and has been in Canada since 2010, came across the personal ad of another gay man on the Internet classifieds portal craigslist.org, who was looking for someone for a one-night stand. On this, Justin gets in touch and arranges a meeting with the advertiser, Luka Magnotta. What he doesn't suspect, Magnotta has already planned his death. Justin's death is a terrible loss for his family, and their loved ones can't get over it. For a Chinese friend of Jun Lin's, it's clear: "Luka Magnotta didn't just kill this one person, he destroyed the entire family."

Magnotta, now referred to in the media only as the "Porno Killer," the "Canadian Psycho," or the "Butcher of Montreal," is now at the center of a global manhunt. In early June 2012, he is said to have been first spotted in a café as well as in a hotel in Paris. On June 4, 2012, the killer is discovered at lunchtime in an Internet café in the Neukölln district of Berlin - sitting there, relaxed, reading the latest reports about him in the various online newspapers on the computer with the number 25. The employee, who works in the Internet café's after-hours tobacconist's, is certain when he catches sight of his guest: It's the man from the newspaper photos! He immediately runs outside the store door onto the street and looks out for a police patrol; he knows that patrols are often carried out here. Gesticulating wildly, he stops the next police car - but the occupants simply don't take the agitated man seriously. Only the police officers in the next patrol car he stops believe him and immediately call for reinforcements. The arrest proceeds calmly and unspectacularly. One of the seven police officers politely asks the man, who is now reading a newspaper, if he is Luka Rocco Magnotta? The man denies at first, claiming not to know the name. The police officers persist and follow up. They keep a close eye on the man. In case his mood changes from one moment to the next and he tries something heedless, they don't want to lose any time. If only to avoid endangering the other people in the Internet café. But he remains unexpectedly calm; Magnotta doesn't seem to even consider making an escape attempt or any other desperate act. Then his eyes suddenly light up for a split second; a mischievous smile plays around his lips, and he now replies to the policeman's demand: "OK, you've got me."

While Magnotta is in German prison awaiting extradition to his home country, Jun Lin's second hand and other foot are now turning up in Canada. Staff members at two different Vancouver elementary schools, who are processing incoming mail that day, initially suspect no evil when they turn to the packages, even though an unpleasant odor surrounds them. Looking inside, however, will haunt them for the rest of their lives. One package contains a hand, the other a foot - both in a state of advanced decomposition. The skin is greenish pale, the tissue underneath has already liquefied and partially leaked. Dark green veins run through the body parts. The only thing that remains unexplained is the location of the Chinese student's head. There is still no trace of it. What did Magnotta do with it?

On June 18, 2012, a military plane lands in Quebec and the murderer sets foot on Canadian soil once again. At the airport, Magnotta is already awaited by officials who immediately transfer him to the local detention center. 14 days after the young man's extradition, evidence is received of additional human remains in a Montreal Park, in bushes near a small lake, from walkers. Investigators initially keep a low profile, but two days later finally state: yes, the severed head found belongs to Jun Lin's body!

The start of the trial on Monday, September 29, 2014, causes a huge surprise: After Magnotta had previously always pleaded "not guilty" to essential charges in hearings before the magistrate, he and his lawyer now unexpectedly choose a completely different strategy. This time, the "Canadian Cannibal" pleads guilty - at the very least - to desecration of corpses, dissemination of obscene material, and harassment of high-ranking politicians by sending packages of body parts. However, there were no political messages or demands contained therein. In view of the overwhelming evidence, his defense attorney believes he has little choice. Magnotta insists that he is "innocent" of the murder. The primary goal of his defense attorney Luc Leclair is to spare him the maximum sentence - life in prison. That's why the question of Magnotta's sanity takes on central importance for this trial, which the press is already calling "Canada's trial of the century." He and his defense attorney point out that Magnotta has a long-standing, serious mental disorder, which is why he was not sane at the time of the crime. For the public prosecutor Louis Bouthillier, this is a purely protective claim. He is sure: the defendant only faked the symptoms of the personality disorder. The man is fully capable of understanding and therefore guilty, after all he planned the crime six months in advance.

In fact, no psychiatric report on the murderer Jun Lins is commissioned. Experts in the media are therefore already speculating that Magnotta's refusal is possibly an indication of a severe narcissistic personality disorder. Such people believe they are allowed to do anything, lie, steal - they lack empathy and are only concerned with their own advantage. In the so-called malignant narcissism, even such a monstrous act as a cruel murder would be allowed, if one so burns oneself into the memory of people for all eternity like a dark genius. To explain this uniqueness with a "banal" mental disorder is not up for discussion for a narcissist.

On December 23, 2014, almost exactly 4 years after the first cat killer video was posted on YouTube, the jury finds Luka Rocco Magnotta guilty on all counts of the indictment. In his final plea, the defendant finds no words of remorse for killing the young student. This hurts especially the father of the killed, who follows every day of the trial in the courtroom. The presiding judge imposes a life sentence on the murderer; however, he grants him the possibility of parole after 25 years in prison. In his reasoning, the judge emphasizes that Magnotta, although mentally ill, is still fully capable of guilt. The 32-year-old defendant motionlessly listens to the chairman as he reads out his verdict.

In 2016, Luka Magnotta makes headlines again from the maximum-security Port-Cartier prison. He once again places a personal ad - just like when he met his victim Jun Lin. This time, however, he's looking for a partner for life on a dating portal specifically for prisoners, Canadian Inmates Connect.

"Seeking single man, between 28 and 38 years old, white and in shape. Someone who is loyal, preferably educated, financially and emotionally stable, for a committed long-term relationship. If you think you could be my prince charming, send me a detailed letter with at least [two] photos. I will only reply to those I think are compatible. Please only send serious letters. All inappropriate letters will be thrown away."

Thirty-four-year-old Anthony Jolin, a murderer like Magnotta, feels the appeal of this. Jolin has committed numerous crimes over the years, including an armed bank robbery in which Kelly Wilneff, a Halifax teenager, was executed by him. While serving a six-year prison sentence, he and a fellow inmate stabbed another inmate in the shower in 2003. Jolin is described as a "violent pimp type" and a supporter of "white supremacy." He is also serving his sentence for the shower room murder at Port-Cartier.

The two quickly become close as they communicate by letter, email and phone. To what extent rumors are true that Magnotta even possessed a smuggled smartphone for at least a while is unclear. He allegedly maintained several social media accounts in the meantime, but they were deleted again.

After Magnotta and Jolin got engaged, they were basically entitled to officially visit each other on set days and spend a few hours together in a private love cell. The long-term visiting rooms, which are slightly larger than a normal cell and have a shower, provide an undisturbed and relaxed visiting atmosphere.

On Monday, June 26, 2017, the two will say "I do. The newlyweds want to spend their wedding night all to themselves in the love cell, without supervision, as Canadian law requires for incarcerated wedding couples - but the correctional facility does not allow this.

Luka Magnotta's maid of honor is his mother, Anna Yourkin; she still believes in her son's innocence. In 2018, together with her co-author Brian Whitney, she published a book about her son entitled "My Son, The Killer: The Untold Story of Luka Magnotta and >1 Lunatic 1 Ice Pick<". In it, she describes, among other things, how her son spends his time in prison: there are movie nights for the inmates. Each inmate even has his own television in the detention room to relieve boredom. Magnotta likes to play video games.

The killer takes drawing classes and exercises a lot. But he no longer takes any medication.

There is nothing so confining as the prisons of our own perceptions.

- William Shakespeare (1564-1616)
English playwright, poet and actor - .

CHAPTER 3

The die is cast

Bored, the salesman looks at the hands of the clock, which on this day only seem to move as if at a snail's pace. Time slips by tenaciously; seconds stretch into hours as the man longs for the end of the day on this November 21, 1989. He is grateful for every customer who finds their way into the gun department of the Montreal Checkmate Sports store - like the young man who is now examining the displays with interest.

...He's in his mid-twenties at the most, the gun salesman guesses; the still visible acne alone suggests that the slim guy with the dark, slightly frizzy hair is not long out of puberty. He gives an almost happy impression as he looks around the store; as if he feels completely at ease here. Apparently, this customer also knows what he wants, the salesman is pleased to note. The man, who is about 1.77 meters tall, with a frozen smile on his face and a wide-eyed expression, is looking at a Ruger Mini-14 Rifle on the shelf, which earns him an appreciative glance from the salesman. A semi-automatic rifle, .223 caliber, with up to 50 rounds in the magazine. Lightweight - but deadly accurate, even at longer ranges - the reason why the Mini-14 enjoys particular popularity in Canada. Special police tactical units, so-called SWAT teams, as well as military units now also appreciate the rifle, which was originally used for hunting coyotes and deer because of its enormous penetrating power.

... "The ammunition for it is very effective," the salesman explains to the young man, who seems to know something about guns. "The entry wound is really very small, but the exit wound is all the bigger for it." The somewhat reserved dark-haired man nods, then puts the unloaded, semi-automatic rifle to the test. Slowly, as he learned from his paratrooper uncle, he searches for the pressure point and then swivels to the side, stops and takes aim at an imaginary target.

... "What do you want to hunt?" the salesman inquires.

... "Just small game," Marc Lépine replies with a strange smile before lowering the Mini-14 once again.

Even when little Gamil Rodrigue Liass Gharbi was born on October 26, 1964, his parents' marriage was already showing signs of minor disruption. His mother Monique Lépine had turned almost her entire life upside down for the attractive and successful businessman from Algeria. The daughter of a Montreal bank manager met 30-year-old Algerian Rachid Liess Gharbi in 1962 and immediately fell in love with the tall, confident man. At the time, Monique was working as a nurse, although she had previously planned to become a Catholic nun. By 1963, wedding bells were ringing, which Monique's parents received with rather moderate enthusiasm. Monique's husband Rachid Liess was not only very good-looking, but also incredibly eloquent, which is why he quickly rose to become an exceptionally successful salesman. The Gharbis' lifestyle in the mid-sixties was accordingly: they owned a fancy house, big cars, and were the center of lively parties with a large number of guests.

...The Gharbis were a particularly model family; especially when, after little Gamil Rodrigue, a little girl was also born in 1964: his sister Nadia. For Monique, however, the public appearances became more and more of a real torment, for her husband Rachid hardly missed an opportunity to meet women in an inappropriate manner. He got so close to them that he could rub his private parts against them while dancing. Eventually, he no longer manages to suppress this impulse when riding on public buses. The cause of this behavior of Rachid Liess was mainly the fact that he simply does not respect women, something that even the acquaintances of the Gharbis perceive. The Algerian also begins to treat Monique more and more like a subordinate and eventually even maltreats her with physical violence. His personal maxim is: women are the servants of men. The father of the family becomes increasingly brutal; he throws empty shot glasses in his wife's face and slams her against a stone wall several times in a row. If at dinner she first puts something on the children's plates and only then on Rachid's, it will drive him up the wall. For trivialities and sometimes even in the presence of other people, the man loses his temper. More and more often, Monique therefore retreats to the basement of the house, where she waits, trembling, for the father to calm down again.

...Her two children, Gamil and Nadia, also fall victim to Rachid Liess Gharbi several times. He does not shy away from physically chastising them for trivial things. All it takes is for the children to sing too loudly or forget to say "good morning" to their father when they get up. After punishment, Monique is not allowed to comfort her children.

... In 1971, Gharbi leaves his family and the following year Monique files for divorce. She is not only granted custody of the two young children but is also allowed to stay in the family apartment in one of Montreal's wealthy neighborhoods. At the divorce hearing, Rachid Liess Gharbi denies the accusations made against him, but numerous witnesses confirm Monique's stories. Still, she does not want to deprive the children of their father, so after the divorce she allows him to see Gamil and Nadia once a month, under strict conditions - an offer that her ex-husband does not accept.

...Monique Lépine begins to work in her old profession as a nurse. From the beginning, she invests a lot of time and energy to refresh her knowledge and to be able to advance in her profession. Along the way, she attends numerous professional seminars to further her education. Until Gamil and Nadia are old enough to be left on their own, they are looked after by relatives and friends. The little boy especially loves spending time with his uncle, who used to be a paratrooper in the U.S. Army. Here the little boy learns how to operate and shoot a gun.

...In 1975, Monique Lépine is of the opinion that something is going wrong in her small family. She starts psychotherapy with her children. After completing treatment in the summer of 1976, Monique relocates with Gamil and Nadia to a small house in rural Pierrefonds. The shy seventh grader with the dark curls, who always hides his face under a baseball cap, must therefore change schools. This is not at all easy for him, but in return he meets a real friend for the first time in his life: Jean Bélanger. The model student, however, wants nothing to do with the other kids at the school.

...In 1977, Gamil and Jean are in the 8th grade, the reserved boy tells his friend a serious decision during the lunch break: He wants to take his mother's last name. In addition, he wants to change his first name as well. Together, the boys confer, and Gamil decides to call himself Marc Lépine from now on. He is now 14 years old. From this moment on, he signs all his classwork only with his self-chosen name and also wants to be addressed by his peers only in this way. Neither his mother nor his teachers can dissuade the teenager.

...Jean and Marc spend most of their time in the cellar of the Bélanger family's house, tinkering with electronic scrap. Marc in particular proves to be very skilled and clever at this. At that time, his big dream is to be an engineer one day. The two boys are also fascinated by weapons and the subject of war. They occasionally visit an army store and browse through the displays. Sometimes they shoot at pigeons with their air rifles. Marc proves to be an exceptionally good shot. Thanks to training by his favorite uncle, he rarely misses his intended target.

...Life at home with the Lépines, on the other hand, is becoming increasingly problematic. While Monique Lépine works and completes her advanced studies on the side, she has given Marc the task of doing the housework and taking care of his little sister Nadia. In return, and because he can't find a summer job, he receives a small allowance. But the two siblings are like fire and water. The teenagers get into loud conflicts more and more often. Nadia does everything she can to annoy and provoke her brother. At every opportunity she calls him by his old name, which he hates so much; it's always Gamil, Gamil, Gamil ... Since Monique Lépine has the impression that Marc lacks a male role model, she turns to the "Big Brothers Association" in 1978 and asks for support. The "big brother" who then enters Marc's life is a quiet man in his mid-forties who quickly befriends his protégé and his buddy Jean. They do a lot together and "Big Brother" even gives the boys brand new, expensive electronic equipment. In 1981, the arrangement ends abruptly, the reason unclear. At first, Marc says the man fled to Europe; then he claims "Big Brother" is gay and has been hitting on little boys.

...Shortly after the disappearance of his "big brother", Marc is now 17 years old, the teenager wants to join the army. In downtown Montreal, he visits a recruiting office. The boy is turned down; in the justification, a military official notes only in a terse word "unsuitable." Marc interprets the rejection for himself. Later he says that he was found to be " socially unsuitable ". Another relocation follows: His mother wants to live closer to the St. Jude de Laval Hospital. Here she holds the post of director of nursing. She finds an apartment in St. Laurent, near the Aéroport de Cartierville. This move is a drama for Marc, because it means losing contact with Jean, his only friend. "Marc didn't seem very happy there," Jean Bélanger later describes this time. In fact, Lépine hardly ever leaves his room, always sitting in front of his old computer and surrounding himself with books and old electronic parts. In the fall of 1982, he enrolled in a science course at CEGEP St. Laurent (Collège d'enseignement général et professionnel, or General and Vocational School) in preparation for the engineering degree he had longed for. However, the previously always good student suddenly shows clear weaknesses. In the first semester, he even fails two courses. In the second semester, things finally start to improve, but then Lépine unexpectedly changes his career choice - one of many spontaneous changes that follow. In 1983, he switched from pure science to a course in applied electronics but dropped out in January 1986. This time, the vocational student was about to graduate. Lépine simply stopped showing up at the vocational school from one day to the other. He does not give reasons for this surprising decision. A department head later reported a conversation with the young man in which Marc told him he would rather attend the École Polytechnique (in English: Polytechnic University) of Montreal.

...Evidence shows that Lépine visited the prestigious university for the engineering department on September 11, 1985, to shop with the student body. This experience must have triggered something in Marc, because a little later his grades at CEGEP noticeably deteriorate. In fact, Lépine applies to the École Polytechnique for a place at university in 1986. But in response to his application for admission, he received a rejection letter directly due to the fact that he lacked proof of two required courses at CEGEP. This rejection seems to be a hard blow for the young technology fan, for now he does something completely unexpected: he simply abandons studying altogether and looks for a job in the cafeteria kitchen of the St. Jude de Laval hospital, where his mother holds an influential position. His colleagues at St. Jude de Laval shun Lépine as much as he shuns them; Marc is constantly on edge, doing all the work at a maddening pace, which results in him constantly breaking things. His attempts to be funny also go awry. As the haze of food and the heat in the kitchen aggravate his already severe acne, Lépine is put to work in the guest room, serving visitors their ordered food. But soon the guests start complaining about the waiter's appearance and Marc, in desperation, begins to grow a beard to conceal his ever-blossoming acne. But it doesn't help - the tousled beard makes the young man look even more unkempt. Only Dominique Leclair, a student who works at the clinic during her summer vacation, is kind to her constantly nervous colleague. At one point, she even asks him why he doesn't have a girlfriend. At first Lépine is angry and hurt by the question, then he confesses to Dominique Leclair, "I've asked a lot of girls out, but they've all refused. I know so many girls, but they don't go out with me. I don't look good ..." That the exceedingly shy young man could be in love with her at this time, is something the student does not think about.

...On July 1, 1986, Lépine moves out of his mother and sister's house. His first apartment of his own is a modern one-bedroom apartment in a 24-unit apartment block in Laval, a suburb of Montreal. The only luxury of the top-floor apartment is a small balcony. Since Lépine doesn't smoke or drink, doesn't use drugs, and doesn't have a girlfriend, he can easily afford the rent for the apartment on his salary from the clinic cafeteria and save a little money on a regular basis. The neighbors have no problems with Lépine, who always pays his rent regularly.

...At some point, Lépine again loses his job at the hospital, about which he appears very bitter. Jean Bélanger's first girlfriend, with whom Lépine also has a very good and close relationship, questions him about how it happened at a reunion: "He said he made a little mistake during his three-month probationary period, and they told him to get lost as a result." But what upsets the young man much more than just losing his job is one very specific detail: "He told me he was fired by a woman and another woman took his place."

...When the winter semester begins for Dominique Leclair in the fall, Lépine also makes another of his professional U-turns. This time, he enrolls at CEGEP Montmorency, taking courses in mass communication, algebra and politics - and successfully completing them. This experience seems to give Lépine such a boost that he takes the entrance exam to the Control Data Institute in Montreal. A very renowned computer school, which has the particular advantage that all students work alone and for themselves on their computers. Lépine, the quiet guy with the baseball caps, passes the entrance exam with flying colors and starts the course in March 1988. Everyone who knows him assumes that he will now make another attempt to get into the École Polytechnique after all. Geographically, Lépine is already moving close to his dream university; his next apartment on Rue de Bordeaux in a typical working-class neighborhood is just five kilometers away. The Control Data Institute and his mother's new apartment are also just a few blocks away. This cheap second-floor place, which Lépine shares with an old high school acquaintance, will be his last.

...Marc gets the small bedroom, which he paints turquoise together with his mother Monique. His numerous belongings make the room look decidedly chaotic. On the desk in front of the window with a view of a red brick wall and above-ground telephone cables is his computer, and next to it are lots of electronic parts.

The student's books are piled everywhere, in some cases up to the ceiling. He even deposits them in his closet. In addition, there are numerous video cassettes; most of them are recorded war films. He needs them to research the "strategic aspect," as Lépine explains to his roommate. One of the two art prints on the walls also depicts a war scene.

...While many of Lépine's acquaintances assume he intends to apply to the École Polytechnique one more time, the student plans to join the army. At this point, another of Lépine's traits becomes increasingly apparent: misogyny and sexist views. His roommate resents these remarks, but he believes the reason is that Lépine is simply unable to find a girlfriend. Nor does he get closer to Sylvie Drouin, whom Marc meets in February 1989 during an evening chemistry update class at CEGEP Vieux Montréal. The young woman finds Lépine quite attractive at first, and she asks him to be her lab partner. Because she also asks him to help her with her homework, they meet a few times outside of class. Lépine treats his fellow student extremely disrespectfully most of the time; is very harsh with her. Things get downright creepy when he shows up in chemistry class with a newspaper clipping about a female police officer and complains bitterly. He believes that women should not be allowed to join the police force. In response to lab assistant André Tremblay's retort that there are a large number of female officers on the Montreal police force, Lépine argues, "So far, I've only found the names of six women in the newspaper articles." Apparently, he has done intensive research on how many names of female police officers are mentioned in the local newspapers. His roommate also has to listen to heated tirades about the monstrosity of women working in "male" jobs.

...In March 1989, Lépine drops out of the course at Control Data. He tells the director of the institute simply "that he would change his career." To Sylvie, who has managed to get an engineering place at the Université du Québec a Trois Riviéres (in English: University of Quebec in Trois Riviéres), Lépine claims he will also be studying this fall - at the École Polytechnique. At the end of the summer, his roommate moves out of the shared apartment with Marc.

...On September 5, 1989, Lépine applies for a permit to purchase firearms and receives the authorization without any problems. In October 1989, he visits the campus of the École Polytechnique on a total of three occasions. On the last day of October, he mingles with students in the cafeteria on the second floor of the engineering school. A few weeks later, Marc purchases the Ruger Mini-14 Rifle, complete with a hundred rounds of ammunition, from Checkmate Sports in Montreal. To hunt small game, he tells the gun salesman.

One day later, Marc Lépine is seen again at the École Polytechnique - this time in the administration pavilion. More visits follow. On each of his visits, the young man continues to unobtrusively familiarize himself with the premises and grounds of the École Polytechnique. On December 5, 1989, Lépine showed up at a car rental agency in the afternoon and rented a car.

...Neither his landlord is surprised that he does not receive the rent on time for the very first time in early December; nor Lépine's mother, who receives her present from her son several weeks before her birthday.

...On December 6, 1989, a Wednesday, the weather is cold and uncomfortable. The day is gray, icy drizzle falls steadily from the overcast sky. Marc Lépine is on his way to the École Polytechnique in the afternoon with the rented car. He parks the car in a towing area, then walks through the rain to the engineering school building.

...On this day, there is a very special atmosphere at the École Polytechnique. It is the last day of classes before the Christmas break, before the exams are written during the semester break. After a long, intensive semester, the students, the lecturers and also the administrative staff all feel exhausted and ready for vacation. In addition, there is a certain pre-Christmas and end-of-year mood. The cafeteria on the first floor is cheerfully decorated with streamers and balloons, and a large garland with "Happy New Year" hangs on one wall.

...On this day, Marc Lépine is wearing blue jeans, work boots, a dark jacket and, of course, his trademark baseball cap. He almost looks a little like someone who is out hunting. With him he carries a green plastic garbage bag that reveals nothing about its contents. Between 4:00 p.m. and 4:40 p.m., he is noticed in the registrar's office. He is sitting on a bench in the entrance area, right next to the door. The way he positions himself there is remarkable; it seems as if he deliberately wants to make it difficult for students to enter the room. No student speaks to him- he doesn't speak to anyone either. The only thing Lépine does is hold his green plastic bag. Finally, one of the administrative staff comes up to Lépine and kindly asks him if she can help him in any way. Without saying a single word, he gets up and leaves. Five minutes later, at 4:45 p.m., the young man finds himself in a corridor on the third floor. Here he leans against one of the walls and once again attentively and wordlessly observes the hustle and bustle in his surroundings.

...At about 5:10 p.m., Marc resolutely sets off for his first destination, which is on the second floor. Lépine walks purposefully through the labyrinth-like second floor, through hallways and lounges, past kiosks with snacks, drinks and stationery. Room 230 is the only seminar room on this floor, hidden behind photocopiers and numerous steel doors. Only those who know it will find the room at the end of the narrow, winding corridors. But Lépine has prepared thoroughly in recent weeks.

...In the seminar room at this time, students are giving a presentation to a mechanical engineering class. At first, none of the 62 people present notice the newcomer, who looks as if he has simply arrived late for his class. He stands at the door with a strange, mask-like smile. Only when Lépine approaches to within a meter or two of the students in the front row and orders everyone to stop what they are doing do the 60 students and the two professors register him. Eric Chavarie, one of the presenters, notes that Lépine "was smiling ... He was very calm." Since it is the last class of the semester and the supposed student is obviously in a good mood, everyone thinks it is a joke and talks in a relaxed and boisterous manner. An end-of-semester joke, what a great idea! But then Lépine fires a shot into the ceiling of Room 230 - the strange smile still playing around his lips. Now he finally has the attention he craves, and demands, "Split up! Girls on the left and boys on the right." But no one moves; some even think they are just blanks. Only when Lépine repeats his order, movement comes to those present - but in a different way than he had intended in his military plan. Two students hide behind columns. Two groups do indeed form in the seminar room - but they are mixed. So Lépine repeats his instruction one more time and finally it is as he imagines. When he has separated the women into one unit, he orders the men to leave the room. They are so disconcerted that they obey and go outside the door.

...Now Lépine turns to the female students. There are a total of nine women standing nervously and confused in front of him. He is directly between them and the door, so that an escape attempt is impossible. No one would be fast enough to get past the young man with the self-loading rifle. Then a strange conversation ensues: Lépine asks the nine female students if they know why he is here? - Nathalie Provost musters all her courage and answers, "No." "I came to fight against feminism," Lépine explains to her. "Look, we're just women studying engineering," Provost counters, hoping to convince him of the innocence of the nine female students. Lépine interrupts the young woman and starts shouting, "You're all a bunch of feminists!"-then he opens fire.

From left to right, he shoots a volley with his Ruger at all nine students. Suddenly, a smoky smell fills the classroom; stifled, short screams can be heard. Lépine fires a total of around 30 rounds. Nathalie Provost slumps like a rag doll with a wound to her lower leg and one over her left eye. Six other female students, all around 21 years old, are dead on the spot; they lie on the floor in slowly enlarging pools of blood. Outside Room 230, their male fellow students turn on their heels in panic and flee headlong.

...After Lépine has successfully completed this part of his plan, the spree killer continues his war campaign. He goes to the corridor on the second floor and, 30 meters away from room 230, meets some people standing by the photocopiers. Without bothering to say anything, Lépine fires at them. Three people instantly sink to the floor injured before they understand what is happening to them. Others present run away in panic. When Lépine is past the copiers, he turns around, the wall behind him, and fires into the hallway toward Room 230. Everything looks like a typical scene from his beloved war movies.

... As early as 5:12 p.m., the first emergency call comes into the control center: "There is a hostage situation, shots are being fired, and many people are injured!" After that, Montreal's emergency call system almost breaks down due to the large number of calls. But even the fastest help would come too late, for Lépine acts with great determination and precision, as if it were clockwork. While the police are still gathering and trying to coordinate further action, Lépine continues his path of destruction through the École Polytechnique.

...In the office of the finance director, the newly married employee Maryse Laganiere just manages to lock the door from the inside. She hears the attacker leaving and thinks she is safe. However, the moment she turns to the inside of the office, she stares into the face of a man wearing a baseball cap at the opposite window. Lépine shoots the woman twice, hitting her in the head. Mortally wounded, Maryse Laganiere collapses on the floor of the office.

...Lépine now roams through the now deserted second floor foyer and uses the escalator to get to the first floor. Once downstairs, he heads for the cafeteria. He can still see a group of fleeing people running through the front door of the self-service restaurant, which then slams shut from the inside. The gunman pushes the door open with one hand and immediately opens fire again. A .223 caliber bullet hits Polish-born Barbara Klueznik in the lower back. The force of the bullet ruptures the freshman nursing student's left kidney, pancreas, spleen, diaphragm, liver, heart and left lung. In addition, the sixth and seventh ribs shatter before the bullet exits the left side of the chest. In the process, Barbara Klueznik's body twists in such a way that the next bullet enters her left breast head-on and exits from her back.

...The neurophysiologist Witold Widajewicz, husband of Barbara Klueznik, is standing at the food counter looking at the display when the fugitives run into the cafeteria. They sweep the stunned man away and push him into the kitchen. Now everyone is lying on the floor seeking shelter. The cook guards the door to the kitchen with a sharp knife in his hand, while everyone trembles for their bare lives. Widajewicz does not understand what is going on. He has no idea that his own wife is already dead.

...Meanwhile, Lépine continues his march of destruction through the cafeteria on the ground floor. Those who cannot flee in time seek makeshift cover behind thin plastic chairs or scuffed tables and pray for rescue. The gunman calmly strolls through the cafeteria, firing a few shots here and there before finally leaving the premises through a second entrance door. He kills a total of three young women - one student is seriously wounded.

...Soon three police cars arrive at the scene. The officers immediately organize a cordon around the École Polytechnique, then wait for the specialists to arrive so that the experts can coordinate further action.

...Meanwhile, Lépine goes to the third floor to continue his work of devastation. In the foyer, he first wounds three unsuspecting female students - then kills them. The shooter walks down the corridor to Room 311, where a technical materials class is being held. So far, no one in the room knows what is going on at the École Polytechnique. Here, too, the usual end-of-semester presentations are now taking place. Everyone is taken aback when the door opens, and a man enters. In his hand he holds his Ruger rifle. The fellow students remain motionless. The next moment, Lépine opens fire. The student Maryse Leclair collapses, wounded by bullets. Six of her ribs are shattered, bone splinters have perforated her lungs.

...Two professors and 26 students instinctively take cover under tables like frightened animals. "We were trapped like rats," 21-year-old Eric Forget describes the situation in shock. Bullets whiz through the air. The shooter streaks along the wall to the left and peers under the rows of seats. He kills four women with his semi-automatic rifle. Student Annie Turcotte lies on the floor between two rows of seats, moaning and screaming for help as blood flows from her body. Two shots have hit her in the torso - her once white blouse is now soaked in blood.

... As Lépine reloads, there is a brief pause in the volley of bullets-an eerie silence falls in the seminar room. Maud Haviernick and Michèle Richard take the chance and run towards the door, but Lépine shoots both women before they can reach the exit. In the next moment, the rampaging man jumps onto a chair and begins to slowly stalk across the rows of tables. If he suspects a woman under one of the tables, he fires at her.

... Next, Lépine goes to the badly wounded Maryse Leclair, who is lying on the podium at the head of the room, whimpering for help and gasping for air in a pool of blood. Lépine draws his hunting knife. The blade flashes briefly in the light of the ceiling lamps, then he stabs the defenseless woman three times. One blow hits her right in the heart. Maryse falls instantly silent - the young student is dead.

...Lépine takes one deep breath, then carefully places the blood-stained knife on the desk that professors normally use to store their teaching materials. Next to it, the shooter places an empty magazine before removing his trademark baseball cap. He thoughtfully places the cap next to the other items on the table. Then Lépine takes a seat at the desk and slowly removes his jacket. A large skull is emblazoned on the front of the sweater he is wearing that day. Highly concentrated, he now begins to wrap his jacket around the barrel of the Ruger. When it feels right, Lépine takes another deep breath and whispers to himself: "Oh, shit. Then the very last shot of the day rings out. At 5:20 p.m., the mass murderer blows off his own forehead bone with his own gun. He is killed instantly.

...The rampage, which achieves sad fame as the "Montreal Massacre," lasts twenty minutes. In total, the rampage killer murders 14 women and wounds 13 other people, including 4 men. ...Meanwhile, the police officers in front of the university in the cold drizzle are still waiting for the district commander in charge. In the meantime, there are seventeen vehicles and 28 officers in front of the building - but no one dares to enter the engineering school. It is not until 5:35 p.m. that the specialists and the district commander in charge of the operation finally arrive on the scene. At the same time, the news leaks out that the spree killer has executed himself - a minute later, the police storm the building.

...In room 311 on the third floor, the officers discover the body of Marc Lépine. When they search his belongings, they discover a suicide note totalling three pages in one of his jacket pockets. In addition, the spree killer carries a handwritten note that reads, "Sorry for the mistakes, I only had 15 minutes to write this." Authorities are keeping quiet about the contents of the suicide note.

...A day later, the rental car Lépine rented is found in a restricted zone near the university. In the car, the investigators discover another letter from the dead man. It was addressed to a friend. It says that the real reason for the massacre can be found in his apartment. All they had to do was follow the clues left in the apartment. But the policemen discover only a suitcase with computer games and hardware.

...The provincial government as well as the city government of Montreal set a three-day national mourning for the victims. This rampage marks the worst mass murder in Canadian history to date. Reactions in Canada and around the globe vary between grief, bewilderment and sheer anger. Especially for the Montreal families the event is a heavy blow, as many of them are personally affected.

...The autopsy of Marc Lépine reveals that the mass murderer and suicide victim had no alcohol in his blood; there are also no traces of other drugs. But how could it come to the terrible act on December 6, 1989? What drove Lépine to do it? The investigation report explicitly states that Lépine considered women and especially feminists to be his enemies. But as the reappraisal of the Montreal massacre progresses, the focus shifts. For example, some commentators blame the violent action movies and games that the spree killer was so fascinated with. Others point to social ills or the fact that Lépine was born in Canada but had an immigrant background and did not feel he belonged. Still others assume that the Montreal massacre was simply the act of a lunatic. A psychiatrist, who interviewed Lépine's family and was given access to the investigation files, suspects that the shooter had a serious personality disorder. Such acts are typical for men with a narcissistic problem, who on the one hand have fantasies about their grandiosity and successes as well as an immense need for recognition, but on the other hand extremely suffer from rejections and failures. They then resort to forms of violence with above-average frequency. Since Lépine had identified women, and especially feminists, as the ones responsible for his failure, his act of revenge had followed. This ultimately gave him the fame he had always secretly longed for. Another psychiatrist's theory, on the other hand, says that Lépine suffered brain damage from his father's violent acts, which caused him to become psychotic.

...Only sometime later the attempts at explanation shift again to what Lépine himself had mentioned as a motive for his rampage and which was already recorded in the investigation report: Anti-feminism. In the meantime, the massacre was clearly judged by criminologists to be a hate crime against women. Lépine did not know any of his victims personally - he killed the students merely because they were women.

...In 1990, Francine Pelletier, journalist and editor of a feminist newspaper, received Marc Lépine's three-page suicide note. Until that time, it had not been released to the public. When Pelletier held the letter in her hands on November 22, 1990, and skimmed the lines, she knew immediately that it was a sensation. For it includes not only the reasons for the rampage, but also a list of 19 prominent women from Quebec whom Lépine also wanted to kill because he counted them as feminists. The journalist is campaigning for the mass murderer's lines to be published in the Canadian newspaper "La Presse".

...The letter opens with the sentence: "I will die on December 6, 1989." There is no blind anger to be discovered in the letters; the author wrote calmly and rationally. Among other things, Lépine makes arrangements for the time after his passing. For example, he asks that his landlord be given the refrigerator from his apartment as compensation for the outstanding monthly rent. The rest of his belongings are to go to his old friend Jean Bélanger. The lines seem almost as if they had been written by a terminally ill person - and in fact Lépine also had his end in mind.

...In his farewell letter, the rampage killer confesses that he has been continuously unhappy for the last seven years - since his mother moved away again, which separated him from his only friend, Jean Bélanger. He also says that his supposed career aspirations were merely feints, since he already "knew his fate in advance." Lépine defends himself against the evaluation of his person as a "crazy killer", rather he is a "rational scholar" whom simply "the feminists always made angry". For him, perfect equality of the sexes is a farce - in his understanding, there can be no equality. And he accuses the feminists of both appropriating the "advantages of women" and at the same time demanding the "advantages of men".

...For the end of his letter the mass murderer chooses a famous Caesar quote: "Alea Jacta Est.

...Life in Montreal will forever be marked by the events of December 6, 1989, which has since been declared a national day of remembrance against violence against women - flags are flown at half-mast on that day. At the École polytechnique de Montréal, silence remains every year on December 6 to commemorate the victims of the rampage; no classes are held. In Montreal, vigils are often held, and discussions are initiated that address violence against women. A memorial to the victims of the slaughter is located just a few steps away from the scene in the Côte-des-Neiges-Notre-Dame-de-Grâce neighborhood. The Canadian capital Ottawa and Vancouver also each have a memorial with the designation "Marker of Change," although the dedications triggered public discussions in each case - they were formulated too politically. The disputed inscription in Vancouver reads: "women who have been murdered by men". It was not removed despite public criticism - however, since then all artworks that could offend certain groups of the population have been banned in Vancouver.

...The event also left its mark on art, music and film: in 2009, the Canadian film "Polytechnique" was released, triggering controversy due to its authenticity. The play "The Anorak" and the death metal song "Montreal Massacre" by the band "Macabre" also deal with the rampage.

...Marc Lépine's sister Nadia Gharbi died of a drug overdose in 1995. Her body is found in a dirty basement apartment in Montreal. His mother Monique does not speak publicly about the murders committed by her son for 17 years. Only after the rampage at Dawson College in 2006, in which one person died and 19 were injured, does she decide to speak out. In 2008, her book is published under the title "Aftermath", in which she tells Marc's story. She suspects that she, as his mother, and his sister Nadia, whom he hates, are the cause of Marc's rage against feminists. With the act he had wanted to take revenge on them.

A thief calls other thieves rogues.

- German proverb-

CHAPTER 4

Slipped through the cracks

(by Marie van den Boom/ Murder Whispers)

The tranquil town of Whitewood is located in Saskatchewan, a province in southern Canada. Its inhabitants proudly refer to themselves as the "Crossroad Community". This nickname is derived from Whitewood's unique location. Here, "In the Middle of Nowhere," two major highways of Canada, Highway 1 and Highway 9, are intersecting.

"In Whitewood, you either stay for a day or forever," residents will joke.

One family that has taken that saying to heart is the Millers. Their idyllic farm sits just off the highways, and visitors are greeted from afar with a sign touting the farm's fresh eggs and delicious pickles.

Lyle and Pam Miller fulfilled their big dream in 2002, buying the 640-acre piece of farmland with the old 1920s farm. A farm of their own with agriculture and lots of animals, with enough space to give their three children a carefree, happy childhood. Pretty much like the comedy "Dr. Dolittle." Except without the actor Eddie Murphy.

Early in the morning, July 23, 2006, 10-year-old Zach is awakened by the crowing of the rooster. Blinking sleepily, he rubs his face in tiredness. The first rays of sunlight cast a golden glow on the lush fields of Whitewood. Outside in the farmyard, you can hear the clucking of the chickens and the wind catching the leaves of the trees and making them rustle.

Even though Zach is still very tired and would have liked to have stayed in bed, he has to get up. "It's no use," the boy mumbles to himself. The animals are waiting and want to be looked after. Whether child or adult, everyone lends a hand here at the Miller's place. Zach's brother, his sister and he have learned that from an early age.

This Friday in July is a fairly warm day in Whitewood. There are only a few scattered fleecy clouds in the sky and by noon the temperature climbs to a pleasant 23 degrees. There's plenty to do on the farm, as usual, and Zach is helping his mother Pam make gooseberry jam. The sweet smell wafts throughout the house.

Just then, a humming noise catches his attention. A car pulls into the yard. Zach drops everything and runs out of the house, curious to see who has just arrived. After all, no one strays to them that often.

Pam also runs after her son and greets the young man who is just getting out of the car. Then she notices the little boy sitting in the passenger seat of the car. Shyly, he looks up at them. "He had to be Zachary's age," Pam thinks to herself, " How nice, maybe he' d have a new playmate."

The stranger introduces himself as Peter Whitmore. He's new in town and traveling with his 14-year-old nephew. Josh starts school here next month and it would be great if he could meet some kids before then. That way, starting over in a strange school wouldn't be so bad.

Zach is happy. Out here in the country, you don't meet new kids very often, and when you do, they're usually gone again after a few hours.

A few days later Peter Whitmore comes to the farm again. Now Zach's father Lyle also gets to know the young man his wife had already raved about. Peter is not here without reason, he needs help. His van has a flat tire, and a rim is also damaged. Lyle, who knows about cars, offers him his help and together the men are able to repair the van. Afterwards, Pam even invites the uncle and his nephew to stay for dinner. After all, the kids get along so well. They arrange for the boys to meet again to play the next day.

Zach is already looking forward to it. That will be fun. There are so many great things to do and discover here in the country. It never gets boring. He has so much he wants to show Josh.

July 30, 2006, a Sunday, begins like any other. First the many animals are taken care of, then the housework is waiting and after that it's finally time to play.

Josh comes over to play as arranged. Zach, who always stands out with his reddish hair and freckles, and the blond, shy Josh are getting along right away. The two boys grab two bikes and explore the neighborhood. Close by is an old farm that they want to check out. It's a perfect adventure playground for romping, climbing and playing hide-and-seek.

Once there, they look around. The garage seems interesting. The boys get off and carelessly throw the bikes on the ground. Carefully, Zach pushes open the door. Inside the garage everything is dark and dusty. The air that hits him is warm, musty, and stale. Cautiously, he takes a step forward and into the darkness.

As soon as he is fully inside the barn, things happen very quickly. Much too fast to realize what is happening.

Zach is suddenly grabbed from behind. He flinches in fright, but the very next moment someone tapes his mouth shut, ties him up and pulls a sack over his head. What is going on here? What is happening to him right now? Is this all a joke?

No, it's not a joke. It's the beginning of a nightmare come true that Zach can't wake up from.

He is completely helpless. Fear and panic paralyze his body. Roughly, he is thrown into the trunk of a van, which starts moving shortly after. Zach hears the engine roar and feels the vibrations. He rolls from left to right; unable to get his bearings. The ride takes what seems like an eternity.

During the never-ending drive, he thinks of his mother, his father, his siblings. He will never see them again. Panic floods his body. Surges over him like a wave and buries him. Over and over, he wonders what his parents are going to think. He is so afraid of disappointing them and is shocked at how this could happen to him. How is he ever going to get out of here?

After about twenty minutes, which seems significantly longer to Zach, the van finally stops. The trunk lid opens, and someone tugs at him; pulling him towards them. Zach struggles as best he can, squirming; trying to scream with his mouth taped shut. But except for a hoarse whimper, no sound comes out of him, and he has no chance against the firm grip of his opponent.

Shortly after, he feels something cold on his neck. Zach breathes frantically, panics again. What is this? Was that it? No.

The attacker puts a cold leather dog leash on Zach and drags the gagged boy into an old, abandoned and run-down farmhouse.

The windows and some doors are boarded up and everything is dirty, dusty and rotten. Nobody has lived here for a long time. There is nothing anywhere around the house. It is very hidden and off the road.

When the bag over his head is finally taken off, he looks around anxiously. Now at the latest, Zach realizes that this is no stupid joke. No one is going to stand in front of him and shout "Surprise! He is sitting on an old bed and his feet are attached to it with ropes. Immediately Zach tugs at the restraints, but the material only cuts further into his skin. Discouraged, he stops what he's doing and now focuses on the man responsible for all of this.

He knows him. It's Peter Whitmore.

Confused and unsettled, his eyes search the darkness. The rotten wooden door of his room is ajar and in the next room he spots another boy. It is Josh, who is also tied to a bed. He looks down at the floor, afraid and ashamed.

The next two days become hell on earth for Zach and Josh, for Peter is not at all a nice, friendly man. He only pretended to be one to trick the Millers. He always had the ulterior motive of getting to Zach.

Everything had been a perfidious plan, which he now finally wants to put into action. He feels this pressure inside him. This desire that he can't fight.

Whitmore repeatedly forces the two frightened boys to watch child porn with him. He abuses and rapes them. When they resist, he hits them. It is an unbridled and raw violence that strikes the innocent children.

Again and again, he threatens them, even at gunpoint. It is their own fault. Peter announces that he will cut them into pieces if they even attempt to resist or flee. After that, he would also kill Zach's family and all those dear to him.

For Zach, the martyrdom is almost unbearable. Many times, he thinks it would be better if he would just die. Then all this would have an end.

The questions in his head don't stop; they circle inside him and keep him awake at night. "When is he going to stop? Why is he doing this to me?" it keeps going through Zach's head over and over again. With all his might, the boy tries to lock Peter out of his mind and thoughts. He closes his eyes and tries to dream himself to another place. Back to the farm. To his parents and siblings. What he would trade to hear the rooster crow early in the morning and smell the scent of gooseberry jam once again.

At night, when Whitmore is asleep and leaves the boys alone, Zach tries to distract himself. He has made friends with the little mice that cautiously crawl out of the vents in the house at night. He shares what little food he has with them and finds some comfort. Animals have always come first for him and his family. So now it is the mice who are with him in this difficult time, giving him strength and courage. He must continue; must fight and must not give up now.

Thus, two days pass that feel like half an eternity for the injured, battered and frightened boys; accompanied by the paralyzing uncertainty and pure fear for their lives.

But on Tuesday, there finally is a ray of hope; a small glimmer of optimism that sprouts up inside Zach.

Outside in the yard, he hears noises. A car approaches and finally stops in front of the barricaded house. Whitmore has heard it, too, and seems increasingly nervous. He jumps up and tries to catch a glimpse of the yard through a gap between two wooden boards.

For Zach, this is the opportunity. He senses his chance, wants to finally break out of the cruel prison and escape his tormentor.

As soon as Whitmore is distracted, he grabs a rusty old saw blade, which he had noticed a few hours ago, and begins to cut through his bonds. Again and again, he rubs it across the ropes, but his progress is slow. The saw is very dull, and it takes forever. Zach is terrified of being discovered by Peter and having to endure the physical and mental torture once again. He simply has to pull through. The adrenaline in his body seems to release unimagined forces in him and finally the rope is cut. At last, he can move normally again. But he is still not out and thereby safe.

Whitmore is still watching the action outside the house, so this is the opportunity. Zach gathers all his courage, jumps up and runs. Panicking, he looks for an exit, but doesn't find one at first until he sees a small opening in the ramshackle wall of the house. Zach sees the sunlight shining through. Without thinking any further, he squeezes through the hole and then runs as fast as his little feet will carry him. Away from the house, away from this terrible place and above all away from Peter.

But he doesn't get very far. An old fence blocks his escape route, but even that can't stop him now. After all, he has already come this far. With his last bit of strength, he manages to kick down the fence and then, exhausted and still full of fear, stumbles onto the path that lies just behind it.

The male and female police officers, who are just outside the run-down farmhouse and about to storm the building, can't believe their eyes when Zach staggers out of the bushes onto the path just a few feet from them and then runs toward them in a panic.

Finally, they find him. For two days, all of Whitewood has been turned upside down. The whole town is frantically searching for the 10-year-old boy.

Zach is picked up by the officers and finally taken to his parents' farm in a squad car. The closer they get to the so familiar surroundings, the more agitated the child is. He doesn't know how to react. How is he supposed to explain all this to his parents?

When the Millers see the police car, they all rush out of the house to receive their beloved Zachary. The last two days have left clear marks on all family members. The terrible fear and the agonizing uncertainty were almost unbearable.

Zach is barely out of the car before he falls into their arms. Everyone is crying with relief and even the experienced investigators have some tears running down their cheeks. After all, something like this doesn't happen every day.

Zach is completely confused and upset. He has experienced so many horrible things over the last 48 hours; endured so many fears and yet the boy can't stop apologizing. He has caused his family so much grief and pain. He is terribly sorry.

But Pam and Lyle interrupt their son. "Enough of that!" If anyone isn't to blame for all of this, it's their little Zachary. The main thing is that he's back with them. That's the only thing that matters. It will be years before the family, and especially Zach, can somewhat come to terms with what they have experienced. The external and, above all, the emotional wounds are too great.

For Pam, it had already been apparent on Sunday afternoon, the day her son disappeared, that something was wrong. When the two boys fail to show up for lunch, she sets off for the nearby old farm after some time. She knows that her son likes to play here and is pretty sure she will find the two boys here right away. But as soon as she gets there, she neither hears nor sees Zach or Josh. The only thing she sees are the two bicycles parked neatly against the wall of the house. No cause for concern yet, though Pam knows her son inside and out. If there's one thing he's not, it's neat. He would never have parked his bike like that.

Flustered, she calls Lyle, who' s out of town and has some errands to run. She tells him about her suspicions. He advises her to inform the police at once.

She does just that. Word of Zach and Josh's disappearance quickly spreads through the small town of Whitewood, and soon the whole neighbourhood is on its feet looking for the two missing boys.

Late in the evening, an "Amber Alert" is issued. This highest alert level serves to make the population aware of a current missing child case as quickly and comprehensively as possible.

The police investigate, and Peter Whitmore is quickly linked to the disappearance of the two boys. Little by little, more and more gruesome details come to light about him, and more questions are raised as to how such a dangerous man could continue to travel the country unmolested.

Peter Robert Joseph Whitmore is a paedophile sex offender with multiple convictions who had already been sentenced to prison five times for sexually abusing seven other children before Zachary and Josh were kidnapped. Despite this, he repeatedly managed to be released early. He slipped through the cracks and was thus able to pursue his atrocities unhindered.

Josh was also kidnapped by him and was not, as Whitmore had claimed, his nephew. His parents had been worried sick about their son for over a week.

Meanwhile, the officers scoured the streets of Whitewood, searching everything for the two missing boys.

Then, on July 31, 2006, a Canadian arrest warrant is issued for Whitmore on suspicion of child abduction.

Everyone is desperately searching for the children, and with each passing hour, hopes of finding them unharmed dwindle.

Pat Beaujot, a farmer from Whitewood, also joins the search. His farm is also just outside of town, so it's a happy coincidence that he drives to the neighboring old farmhouse during his lunch break to search for the boys. The closer he gets to the overgrown building, the more an uneasy feeling creeps over him. Fresh tire tracks are clearly visible on the overgrown path leading to the farm, and even the gate is open. Cautiously, he dares to take a look at the yard. He sees a pile of garbage with some packaging from the fast food chain KFC. It all looks as if someone had been here recently. Shortly after, he notices the blue van parked in a barn. "Isn't that the car of the wanted man, Peter Whitmore?" Pat asks himself incredulously. Should he really have found the kidnapper's hiding place here, and possibly the two boys as well?

Agitated, he drives back to his own farm and tells his wife about his find, who immediately informs the police. Shortly thereafter, Zach runs into the officers, having managed to successfully escape from his tormentor.

Josh, on the other hand, can only be freed after another 10 hours and never-ending negotiations between the police and Whitmore. The latter is finally arrested shortly thereafter.

The children's ordeal has come to an end.

Peter Whitmore is sentenced to life imprisonment at the subsequent trial on July 23, 2007. He pleads guilty to twelve of the fifteen charges - including sexual assault of children with bodily injury and other sexual offenses, kidnapping, threatening to murder, and a child pornography offense.

In addition, a publication ban will be placed on Zach and Josh's names. This is to protect the children.

An incredible burden falls from the victims' families after the verdict. Tears are shed. Still, the mental wounds of Whitmore's heinous acts are far from healed, and their scars will mark the survivors and their family for the rest of their lives.

Zach Miller is 25 years old today. He wants and needs to tell his story. For far too long, he has remained silent.

Today, Zach works as a heavy equipment operator and openly talks about what happened to him 15 years ago. After all, the time after that wasn't easy either. He was bullied at school and repeatedly confronted with what he had experienced.

Zach finds it difficult to trust and allow physical closeness. To this day, he does not like hugs. At night he is plagued again and again by nightmares.

And yet he doesn't give up. He is campaigning to have his name and story published. His greatest goal is to help and encourage as many affected children as possible.

Today, he says, "Up until that point, I was just an average farm boy, but after what happened, I'll never be the same."

Peter Whitmore has the option of applying for parole for the remainder of his prison sentence.

If he does, Zach plans to be at the hearing and do everything in his power to prevent that from happening. "I will be there to protest. We don't need another tragedy like mine."

»O comfort-killing night, image of hell, Dim register and notary of shame, Black stage for tragedies and murders fell, Vast sin-concealing chaos, nurse of blame!«

- William Shakespeare (1564-1616)
English playwright, poet and actor -

CHAPTER 5

Deal with the devil

What if their children find out what kind of person their mother really is? For behind the attractive facade, the good manners, something completely different lies: something disturbing, deeply threatening; even if this is not apparent to the good-looking woman. Only those she really lets into her life are allowed to see into the dark, hidden abyss of her soul. But to outsiders, she is the kind, concerned mother of three delightful children who are growing up cared for.

For Karla Leanne Homolka, it's like being struck by lightning when she sees the incredibly handsome young man in a Scarborough restaurant. On October 17, 1987, the 17-year-old veterinary assistant simply wants to relax and celebrate with her colleague Debbie Purdie after an exhausting professional conference, when the man enters her life, to whom she instantly feels magically attracted. And he feels the same way. The 23-year-old accountant Paul Kenneth Bernardo is also instantly fascinated by the pretty, slim blonde with the long hair who has the Princess Diana look down so perfectly. For both of them, the hustle and bustle of the restaurant with its numerous guests, the hastily running waiters, the clinking of cutlery on dishes has become meaningless in one fell swoop. They only have eyes for each other. The fairy tale of love at first sight, it seems to have come true. The companions of the shock lovers both feel that there is a direct sizzle between the princess Karla and the cultured Paul, who has a good position at the prestigious company Price Waterhouse. The encounter has something animalistic and only a few minutes after the first contact, the two cannot keep their hands off each other. No one is surprised that on this evening of their first encounter, the two make love. But everyone still assumes that it is a one-night stand.

In Karla's eyes, Paul is the absolute dream man. As a child, she owned a plethora of Barbie and Ken dolls, with which she played according to precise rules, according to her specifications. And even then, she had only one dream: she wants to marry a man who is like Ken.

Something also happens that evening with Paul, who is actually dark-haired, but at this point looks like the girlish dream of a California surfer boy with his dyed blond mop of hair. He gets Karla's phone number and address - contrary to his usual habits. Paul can't deny it: he has fallen head over heels in love with the blonde. A fateful encounter. Karla's only flaw in the eyes of the conservative 23-year-old: at 17, she's already no longer a virgin on their first night together. He' s obsessed with the idea of being a woman's first husband.

But that doesn't stop Paul from meeting his dream girl again just 2 weeks later. Although the two lovers live an hour and a half's drive from each other, Paul still travels to see his Karla at least twice a week. The young woman is so in love that she will do anything for her new boyfriend, who quickly rules every aspect of her life: He decides what she should wear, how she should style her hair, what her opinions should be. Once Paul has gained control over the young girl, he begins to humiliate Karla: He insults the slender woman as fat and ugly. He forces her to engage in unusual sexual practices during sex, which Karla actually finds degrading. But even that is no reason for the woman in love to leave her new boyfriend. Rather, she is completely obsessed with the idea of making her "Ken" happy. Her greatest fear of all is losing Paul to another woman. That he still has sex in a very special way with numerous other women in addition to his relationship with Karla; she has no idea of that at this time.

Karla is born into a middle-class family on May 4, 1970, in the Port Credit district, located in the south-eastern province of Canada. The parents Karel and Dorothy Homolka have two more daughters after their firstborn. In 1971 Lori was born. Four years later little Tammy was born. While still in school, Karla begins to work part-time in a pet shop. After graduating from school in 1988, she is hired by a veterinary clinic as an assistant.

Paul Bernardo, who was born on August 27, 1964, grew up under completely different circumstances. His mother Marylin, adopted at a young age by a wealthy Toronto lawyer, is raised in a posh environment. In 1960, she marries a well-off, successful businessman, half-Italian Paul Bernardo. A marriage that Marylin's wealthy adoptive family, who belong to the city's upper class, openly disapprove of. The young couple moves to a middle-class neighborhood in Scarborough. They then have two children, the progenitor David and a girl, little Debbie. Little by little, the dark side of Marylin's husband comes to light: he is violent; repeatedly abuses his wife. Perhaps that's why she finally seeks solace with her former childhood sweetheart for a while. An affair with consequences, as Marylin becomes pregnant and gives birth to a boy. Her husband seems to have no suspicions or is simply not interested, so the child conceived out of wedlock is given the name Paul Kenneth Bernardo in August 1964.

The relationship between the parents of little Paul Kenneth nevertheless deteriorates steadily. Mainly because of the father's habit of sneaking around the neighborhood in the dark and peeking through the windows of young girls to watch them. On top of that, he is convicted of indecently touching and fondling a girl. At home, Bernardo repeatedly abuses Marylin and his children, David, Debbie and Paul Kenneth, over the years. In addition, the man is rumored to have sexually assaulted his daughter. The conditions put such a strain on Kenneth's mother, Marylin, that she becomes depressed. To numb her pain and fill the inner emptiness, the woman begins to continually eat. Soon, the mother of three has put on such massive weight that she is no longer able to take care of her children herself or to do the housework that needs to be done. At this point, her husband quarters her as far away from himself as possible in the house in Scarborough - in the basement.

Despite this unfortunate initial situation, little dark-haired Paul Kenneth charms the people around him with his sweet smile, his friendly, polite and always a little shy manner. At the age of five or six he runs away from home once, a few days later the boy reappears. His brother Dave later mentions that all this time no one asked where Paul was. In the following years, multiple scuffles with neighbor children occur, who like to make fun of the Bernardo family and play tricks on them. Paul Kenneth is repeatedly observed beating other children - on the lawn in front of the house. Otherwise, he has little social contact with his peers. However, he proves to be a child who is absolutely fearless and cares little for his physical integrity during athletic activities.

He is a good student and does not give his teachers any trouble. In his spare time, he is active in the Boy Scouts, where he quickly gains a position of trust, and starts earning extra money early on with jobs outside of school. He's like the perfect kid.

But at 16, Paul Kenneth reveals a different side of himself. A loud argument ensues between him and his mother. Marilyn is so angry with her son that she unceremoniously slams a photo of a man he doesn't know on the table and tells him that he is the result of a fling. This must have affected the teenager quite badly, as from now on the once-perfect child is completely transformed. Although Paul Kenneth remains the friendly young man on the outside, he has lost respect for his mother. He insults her as a slut and a whore. He hates his father because of his pedophilic tendencies, which only become public when the police finally get involved; the relationship with his parents breaks down completely.

In the following years, Paul Kenneth reads many books about communication and manipulation techniques and how to use them correctly to assert his own selfish interests. Soon he is recruited by an American company, Amway, which is repeatedly accused of running a pyramid scheme. Later, young Paul takes a famous televangelist Jim Bakker as a role model, an excellent rhetorician (later also condemned as a fraud), who captivates millions of people with it in the 70s and 80s and uses his speech methods to get girls into bed with all kinds of fanciful stories and otherwise gain advantages. Something that works brilliantly in every way. Girls hang on his every word and are easily persuaded by the supposed Prince Charming to have a one-night stand before he drops his conquests like a hot potato.

During his time at the University of Toronto, Paul is always on the lookout for a rewarding scam to get some quick and easy cash. Due to his dissolute lifestyle, he needs a lot of cash and that can't be earned with normal jobs. He loves prestigious cars, likes to dress well, has a soft spot for nice houses and good food. Paul's sexual fantasies become increasingly extreme over time: he develops a special preference for hard anal sex and submissive women. Bondage sex and beating his sexual partners are also high on his list of priorities. Initially deeply in love with the handsome Paul, the women put up with this for a while until they realize that he is just using them as sex objects. The relationships last a month at most. If his ex-partners pressure him to tell them what he has done to them, Paul threatens them. Having power over women excites Paul, and therefore he is soon looking for the next, ultimate thrill. In the summer of 1986, however, the young man is first called to account for his assaults: he has been harassing the ex-girlfriend of a good friend with obscene phone calls. The woman obtains a restraining order against the 22-year-old.

May 4, 1987, it is a Tuesday, marks an important turning point in the life of young Paul Bernardo. Only a short time after his successful university graduation, he gives free rein to his urges for the first time on the streets of Scarborough. At 21, he combines the experience of humiliation, hard, brutal sex and the thrill of the criminal act that is so arousing to him. That night, he ambushes the first female victim at a bus stop near his own apartment. The surprise attack from the ambush leaves the woman no chance at any moment to successfully defend herself against her attacker. Her desperate resistance comes to nothing. The 1.80 meter tall perpetrator forces her to have anal and oral sex. He talks to her incessantly and tells her what she has to answer - just like a master does with his will-less slave. Then Paul Bernardo releases the young woman and savors the moment of power to the fullest. He feels safe enough not to be afraid that he could be held responsible for the deed. He decides what happens to his victims, how much he humiliates them. This experience must have been like an initial spark for the man who humiliates young women, who are almost still children, in order to increase his own lustful life. Just 10 days later, the next sexual assault takes place. This time Paul goes even further: he rapes his victim directly in front of their house. Unlike his father, who has since been held accountable by the courts, he is not content to just look in their windows at night and hope to watch them undress. Bernardo junior wants the fast, the hard kick. He wants to humiliate his victims, to take revenge on the world of women for his mother's infidelity. On July 27, 1987, he fails for the first time. The woman manages to escape from her adversary unharmed.

In Scarborough, the public can breathe a sigh of relief for a short time, for just as suddenly as the brutal rapist appeared in town, the series of rapes comes to an end. In the meantime, the perpetrator has found the love of his life and regularly visits her in St. Cathrine: Karla Homolka. The relationship is a completely new experience for the young accountant, occasional cheater and rapist, for Karla shares his sexual preferences. More than that, she even fuels his sadistic behavior. During one of their love games, as the blonde is kneeling tied up in front of Bernardo, he asks her what it would be like for her if he were a rapist ...? Despite her well-protected childhood in a caring family, there is only one logical answer for Karla: "That would be cool!"

What hardly anyone even suspects at this point: Karla Homolka also carries a moral black hole in her soul. No one knows how the abyss came about; the young woman has never had to suffer injury or humiliation. At this point, no one suspects how deep the chasm really is.

Karla and Paul get engaged in December 1987, just two months after they met in the restaurant. In the same month, the rapist resumes his rampage in Scarborough. But this time Bernardo is even encouraged to commit the acts by his fiancée. Bernardo moves into Karla Homolka's parents' house shortly after the engagement. Their whole family is thrilled by the young, charming and brilliant-looking junior accountant with the most promising career prospects. However, he keeps quiet about the fact that he has already lost his first, lucrative job after graduation. Karla, on the other hand, knows everything - she is also on the scene when the Scarborough Rapist abuses women. One victim tells the police that she observed a woman filming her brutal rape during the attack - the officers attribute the observation of the rapist to her overwrought imagination and attach no significance to that part of the statement.

It is 1989, and the perpetrator, dubbed "The Scarborough Rapist" by the press, has been at large for two years now; eleven women have already fallen victim to the man. The police take the incidents very seriously and the search for the criminal is pursued at full speed. The whole town is in fear of the criminal. Young women only go out the door alone when it can't be avoided.

However, one of the victims is able to describe the attacker so well that the police have been able to create a sketch with the help of the witness. To others, Bernardo is amused by the resemblance between himself and the likeness on the wanted poster, but it is precisely this circumstance that arouses the police's interest in him. He quickly becomes the target of the investigators. The police rely on the most modern forensic tests. They order DNA tests to be carried out in this case. Paul Bernardo has to go in for questioning and is also forced to give a blood and DNA sample, but at the end of the 1980s it takes months for a DNA sample to be evaluated. Due to the large number of potential suspects, the results will even take several years. Disastrously. The sketch is not published for a long time.

Not even the fact that Paul's ex-girlfriend Jennifer Galligan has repeatedly gone to the police, only to finally report him for rape, abuse and threats after all, is given any particular significance. No one draws a cross connection between that complaint and the man who is part of the suspect pool in the Scarborough Rapist case. In 1990, investigators release the sketch to the public. The police then receive a flood of tips from the public. Again and again, witnesses point out the similarities between the mugshot and Paul Bernardo. Even former work colleagues of the now 26-year-old from the accounting firm Price Waterhouse come forward with information for the police. Making matters worse, Bernardo lives near the crime scenes and drives a white Ford Capri - like one of the victims had seen at the scene.

Karla, in the meantime, is still blinded by love. Although Paul is getting more and more brutal towards her behind closed doors. When Paul wants a drink, she fetches it - immediately and with a smile on her lips. Although Karla tries to read her prince charming's every wish from his eyes, the man becomes more and more disrespectful towards her. He keeps telling her how stupid she is, how ugly he thinks she is and how fat she is. At the same time, he wonders why he actually tells her this over and over again; in his eyes, Karla is far too weak to change anything about her supposed shortcomings. More and more often Paul expresses his contempt for her with beatings. In the meantime, he has an affair and becomes increasingly interested in Karla's younger sister, the beautiful Tammy. She is supposed to still be a virgin; something Karla can no longer offer him. A circumstance that annoys Paul more and more. At night, he secretly sneaks into Tammy's room and begins to masturbate at the sight of the beautiful young woman as she unsuspectingly lies asleep in her bed.

His fiancée is so obsessed with Paul Bernardo at this point that she would literally do anything for him. Her very worst fear is not being able to keep him. She is tormented by raging jealousy of her sister, the virgin. Her fiancé's interest in Tammy has not gone unnoticed by Karla. At some point, the thought germinates in her mind to "give" her little sister's virginity to her dearly beloved Paul.

She already has an idea how to put her plan into action: As an employee in a veterinary clinic, Karla easily obtains anesthetics. Through her work in the medical facility, the woman also has knowledge regarding the mode of action of the various drugs. Karla proposes to first give Tammy the strong sleeping pill Halcion and then to anesthetize her with Halothane, an anesthetic delivered through the respiratory tract, to the point where Paul can take her virginity - while Karla records everything on video. Karla Homolka neglects the fact that a medical breathing mask is required for the correct administration or dosage of halothane. The blonde assumes that a soaked cloth will suffice if she occasionally takes it off Tammy's face.

When Karla Homolka finally tells her adored Paul Bernardo about her special Christmas present, he is beside himself with excitement. He once again tells Karla how much he loves her.

At the first attempt, crumbled Halcion tablets are added to the spaghetti sauce at dinner, but apparently the dosage is not enough. Bernardo doesn't get his turn. On December 23, 1990, one day before Christmas Eve, the perfidious plan is now to be put into action. The house of Karla's family is festively decorated, the smell of freshly baked cookies is in the air. The state fir tree is decorated with red and gold Christmas ornaments and is lit with numerous candles. Their light is reflected sparkling in the Christmas baubles. Paul films Christmas Eve with his new camcorder: the house, the Homolka parents and the three daughters Karla, Lori and Tammy. Throughout the evening, he keeps providing Tammy with cocktails that contain Halcion as well as rum and eggnog. Eventually, the other family members retire and go to bed. This is the moment when Karla and Paul want to put their disturbing plan into action - they sneak into the room of the deeply sleeping Tammy. While Paul rapes Tammy, Karla records everything on video. Every now and then she puts a rag with halothane over her unconscious sister's face so that what is happening to her can't penetrate her consciousness. Finally, Paul goes one step further and orders Karla to sexually assault her little sister as well - the woman doesn't hesitate for a second to obey her fiancé's command.

The tide turns as the sleeping Tammy abruptly begins to vomit. The administration of the halothane in combination with the sumptuous dinner is causing problems, Karla suspects. She doesn't consider that the side effects of an overdose of the anesthetic are serious: Blood pressure drops sharply, the heartbeat speeds up and cardiac arrhythmias occur. In addition, bromide ions released during metabolism can have a toxic effect and cause allergic shock. Tammy's big sister responds as she knows it from the veterinary clinic: she holds her sister at the waist so that the upper part of her body is pointing upside down, so that she can cough up the vomit. But she has no chance and inhales the vomit into her lungs. She suffocates in agony.

Paul and Karla do nothing to save the woman's young life. They don't alert an ambulance and they don't wake the sleeping parents. Instead, the two make love next to the corpse in Tammy's bed. Then the couple dresses hastily, leaving the narcotics in a bag; they stow the video camera with the tape right next to it. The two mop and vacuum in the middle of the night and do laundry, which surprises no one. None of the Homolkas gets up and looks to see the reason for all this. Only after the work is done do Karla and Paul finally call an ambulance. When it finally comes to a stop in front of the Homolkas' house, Karla and Tammy's parents finally get up to see what's going on. The rescue workers do their best to revive Tammy - only at this moment do Tammy's parents realize what is really going on. Their youngest daughter is dead! The paramedics cannot help the girl anymore. Everything looks like Tammy simply suffocated in her sleep due to too much rum and eggnog cocktail in the evening. No one suspects foul play, not even the paramedics - although Tammy's face is clearly burned by the rag containing the halothane.

Only a short time after Tammy's death, the couple moves out of the Homolkas' house. The couple looks for their own small bungalow in Port Dalhousie. Karla's parents are to be able to mourn Tammy in peace - while the engaged couple, in high spirits, are already intensely thinking about a wedding. But Paul's mood quickly changes once again: first Karla's pet, a poison-green iguana, bites her fiancé, to which he reacts drastically: He cuts off the animal's head, grills the remaining body and eats it. Furthermore, Paul is very upset by the outcome of Tammy's loss of her virginity. He repeatedly accuses Karla of being responsible for her sister's death. However, he is particularly annoyed by the fact that Tammy was taken away from him in this way.

Karla therefore unceremoniously tries to get Paul an equivalent replacement; a very personal gift for her dream man. She would do anything to keep him happy. This time, however, it is to be a complete surprise. Her choice falls on an acquaintance Karla met two years earlier in a pet store. The two women were work colleagues before Karla Homolka got the job at the animal clinic. Karla invites the girl, just 15 years old and known only as "Jane Doe," to her home on June 7, 1991. The procedure is similar to Tammy's: Karla sedates Jane Doe by giving her alcohol to drink with crushed Halcion tablets. When the girl is safely drugged, she calls Paul and asks him to come home. Bernardo is thrilled, especially because the girl reminds him so much of Tammy. Once again, the gang rape is caught on video. First Karla gets off on Jane Doe, then the 15-year-old is brutally raped by Paul. When they finally have enough of their perfidious sex games with the unconscious, they put the girl in a bed so that she can sleep off her intoxication there, caused by alcohol and even more narcotics.

The following day, Jane does not feel well at all when she wakes up. She has bad stomach pains; nausea and her private parts are painfully sore. She can't explain the cause of her sudden discomfort.

Paul is so thrilled with everything Karla does for him that he decides to marry her - even though she has minor flaws in his eyes. After all, she is already much too old for his taste, and she is also no longer a virgin. Perhaps this is one of the reasons why he keeps looking for the ultimate thrill.

It is June 14, 1991, a Friday, when Paul finds what he has been looking for so long. On this evening, he is out and about in the town of Burlington, located in the Canadian province of Ontario., to steal car license plates. He needs them for one of his extremely lucrative cigarette smuggling tours, with which he now earns his living. Nevertheless, he seizes the favorable opportunity to commit a new crime when it presents itself. In the early hours of the morning, it is around 2:00 am, he meets 14-year-old Leslie Mahaffy. It is a momentous encounter. The girl with the long hair, fixed braces and cheerful smile is at a wake that night. Together with friends and relatives, Leslie Mahaffy is watching over the coffin of a deceased acquaintance at the funeral home. Afterwards, they have a drink with friends, which is why the girl is much too late on her way home. In order to educate the rebellious teenager, her parents decide to lock the front door. And so, Leslie now stands in front of her parents' house; but can't get inside. She doesn't dare to wake up her mother and father, so she decides to call a friend from the nearby phone booth. She asks the girl for shelter, but she has to refuse her request. In the darkness of the night, the girl goes back to her parents' house, hoping to discover an open window or door somewhere, so that she can secretly get inside the house. Shortly before Leslie reaches her parents' house again, the teenager meets Paul Bernardo, of all people, who seizes the opportunity. With a knife, he forces Leslie to get into his car. He blindfolds the shocked girl with an oblong piece of cloth and drives her to the bungalow in Port Dalhousie. Without waking Karla, begins to bring his dark fantasies into reality. He begins filming the kidnapped girl sitting on the couch, naked and blindfolded. He is full of anticipation of what he is going to do with his defenseless victim that he even gets the good French champagne glasses out of the cupboard in his exuberance, which he ordered specially from overseas for special occasions. He toasts the abductee with champagne in anticipation. Then he rapes her again and again.

The next morning, Karla is beside herself with anger and jealousy. She is particularly angry that Paul wasted the good glasses and the good champagne with Leslie. That is the first thing she looks at when she wants to take the dog out for a walk that morning. But she soon relents and joins in with Bernardo's games. The young girl is at the mercy of the couple for a whole 24 hours. She has to endure every sexual game the two come up with. Not only does Paul engage in brutal anal sex, but Karla also gets off on the girl. In addition, Homolka and Bernardo torture their victim several times. All this time the eyes of the defenseless teenager are blindfolded. Between the individual attacks, they repeatedly give Leslie a teddy bear and order the girl to hold it in her arms. After all, she is still a child, and these need the comfort of their cuddly toys. Bernardo then gives Karla precise instructions on how to abuse the girl while he films. Like a real director in search of the perfect movie scenes, he has his actors act out his wishes right in the bungalow in the respectable middle class neighborhood in Port Dalhousie. Once he is satisfied with the two women, Paul sets to work raping Leslie so violently that she screams in pain. They only end the girl's ordeal after 24 hours. On June 15, 1991, Leslie Mahaffy is murdered. Karla had not been sure whether the blindfold of her victim had not perhaps slipped, and the girl could thereby possibly recognize her rapists. Most likely, however, the life of the always smiling girl with the braces ends to complete the sense of power in Paul and Karla, with the decision of life or death of their victim. According to Homolka, Bernardo is said to have first twice tried to strangle the teenager with a cable, but it did not work. It is unclear whether or not this incident was another torture attack, or a more serious attempt at murder.

Leslie never wakes up on June 16, 1991, in the bungalow in Port Dalhousie. Her heart has simply stopped beating due to an overdose of the anesthetic halothane. Whether the veterinary nurse, Karla Homolka, overdosed this on purpose or it was another accident cannot be determined. Since Karla and Paul are expecting a visit from their family that day, they unceremoniously deposit the body of the maltreated girl in a bedroom located in the basement. Afterwards, with the help of Bernardo's grandfather's circular saw, the couple cuts the corpse into such small pieces that they can easily be poured into cement. Paul Bernardo then sinks these in Lake Gibson near St. Cathrines.

The murderous couple's wedding, held exactly thirteen days after Leslie Mahaffy's murder, takes place at Niagara-on-the-Lake Church. It is a lavish, perfectly planned and organized celebration. Like something out of a picture book. After the ceremony, the bride and groom board a carriage pulled by white horses. Karla's wedding dress alone cost $2,000 (about 1500 GBP). Some jokingly refer to the wedding couple as Barbie and Ken. 150 guests are invited. In addition to expensive champagne, a fine menu is served. Karla's sister Tammy has only been dead for six months at the time of the wedding ceremony; but that certainly did not dampen the spirits of the newly married couple. The unemployed ex-accountant can afford all the luxury of the wedding because of his illegal ventures. He regularly sets off on tours to the USA to smuggle cigarettes from there to Canada. A lucrative source of income since cigarettes in Canada are very expensive to deter people. To camouflage the tours, Bernardo repeatedly steals license plates, which he then mounts on his cars. Just like the night he came across Leslie Mahaffy.

On the evening of June 29, 1991, a strange concrete block is accidentally discovered in Lake Gibson by a couple taking a canoe trip on the lake. It looks like there are pieces of meat encased in it. The man and his wife ask a fisherman repairing his boat on the shore for help. They want to salvage the block so they can take a closer look. Only when they have heaved the heavy concrete block ashore with their combined forces do they realize what a creepy discovery they have actually made. The rock-hard cement encases a calf and a foot. The alarmed police discover more cement blocks in the water of the lake. In total, they recover five concrete blocks. The raised dental status provides important clues to the identity of the corpse, especially the found braces provide the investigators with the final proof: they have found the remains of the missing Leslie Mahaffy!

Meanwhile, Bernardo is looking for the next thrill and his wife does her best to make him happy. First, she invites Jane Doe once again. This time, she hopes, the girl won't have to be drugged to join in the couple's sex games. But the girl refuses - she believes she is still a virgin. This is not how the teenager imagined her fabled "first time." She finds the couple's request suspicious enough to tell her equestrian instructor about their strange advances. Then, the girl confides in her mother. Both strongly warn Jane Doe against the couple; as a result, the visits to Karla Homolka and Paul Bernardo become less frequent, but do not end for the time being - and once again the two resort to halothane in order to be able to use the girl as a sex slave. Only after Jane Doe also experiences problems due to the halothane, Paul and Karla get "cold feet". Due to a slight overdose, Jane's respiratory center stops working. This time Karla reaches directly for the phone and dials the emergency number. But even as the ambulance races on its way to the address given, the young girl's breathing resumes. Karla then orders off the rescue. However, the murderous couple ends contact with Jane Doe as a precaution. Apparently, they don't want to push their luck on this one.

To keep Paul in a good mood, Karla Homolka has to come up with a new entertainment for him. The extent to which fourteen-year-old Terri Anderson, reported missing from St. Cathrines on November 30, 1991, is connected to this is still unclear. For some time there reportedly was another girl they were secretly using for their sexual games, but this one is said to eventually move to Youngstown, Ohio. This situation is extremely unsatisfactory for Paul and his mood becomes more and more unbearable. Once again, the couple is in a crisis. To spice up the marriage, Karla realizes, she must offer Paul something out of the ordinary.

On the afternoon of April 16, 1992, 15-year-old teenager Kristen French is on her way home from school. The tall, good-looking girl with thick, dark hair is a good student. She attends Holy Cross Secondary School in St. Catharines and is well loved there. She is just at the entrance of the Grace Lutheran Church parking lot when she sees a blonde woman standing in front of her car with a road map in her hand. The blonde seems to be looking for something and looks perplexed. When she catches sight of the girl, she asks her for help. Politely, Kristen steps closer to the parked car, in which a man is driving, and takes a look at the map that the driver continues to hold in her hand. Although passers-by are on the road watching everything, Paul Bernardo springs into action. He jumps out of the car, threatens the girl with a knife and forces her to sit in the back seat of the car. Karla then also gets into the car and the three drive off in the direction of Port Dalhousie. None of the passers-by reacts, neither are the kidnappers approached nor does anyone call the police. Everything continues as if nothing had happened.

One thing is different from the second victim of the murder couple: Kristen is not blindfolded at any time. She looks at the perpetrators and has enough time to memorize their faces. Kristen French also gets to see the bourgeois bungalow as well as the

Bernardos' dog, a circumstance that had previously been avoided, which, according to later statements by Karla, cost Leslie Mahaffy her life.

Do Paul and Karla already know at the beginning of the kidnapping of their victim that the young girl should not survive the crime?

The tall girl cooperates with her kidnappers, hoping to increase her chances of survival. But this behavior only incites the Bernardos all the more. Paul lives out his sadistic fantasies to the full, slapping her in the face with his half-erect penis and asking the girl to smile as he does so. Then she has to lie down on the cold floor of the apartment, because Paul now wants to live out his enthusiasm for practices with "golden shower" and "natural caviar". Golden shower is a euphemism for urine, while natural caviar is feces. He does everything to break this strong girl. First, he urinates on Kristen and declares, "You look good covered in pee." - but only to turn around and squat his rear end over her face. However, the attempt to defecate in the middle of her face is unsuccessful. Karla films everything meticulously. These scenes should serve as stimulating memories for later.

The humiliations extend over two days, only then Kristen French dies in agony. Finally, she summons up all her courage and refuses to do Karla and Paula any more favors. In response to the threats, she simply declares, "Some things are worth dying for." She also formulates another sentence with cutting sharpness, which she hurls at Paul: "I don't know how your wife can put up with you ..." The indomitable girl is strangled with the same cable as Leslie Mahaffy - this time it works right away. The girl suffocates. As the killers are invited to an Easter dinner at Karla's parents' home, they simply leave their victim's body in the bungalow. Only after they have completed the Easter meeting does Paul take care of disposing of the dead girl. He deposits the body in a ditch in Burlington.

After the disappearance of Kristen French, the Ontario government decides to immediately form a special task force to pursue the kidnapping at full speed and solve it as quickly as possible. No one yet suspects that the girl is already dead. In fact, the Green Ribbon Task Force quickly receives important clues, such as a Camaro car seen at the scene of the crime. In addition, the name of Paul Bernardo also appears in these investigations, and he is then questioned by two police officers; however, his car does not match. Because he himself indicates that he is one of the suspects in Scarborough, the investigators contact Steve Irwin, the man in charge; but this remains fruitless for the time being.

On April 30, 1992, Kristen's body is found; just three weeks later, it is May 23, 1992, police divers in Lake Ontario also discover the remains of Terri Anderson, but forensic investigators assume that she died of natural causes. She is believed to have drowned, perhaps while boating or swimming in the lake. However, LSD and beer can be detected in the body of the exemplary student. Behind closed doors, the residents of St. Cathrines say that her father was known to deal drugs on occasion. The girl's death is not followed up.

At this point, the investigation into the "Scarborough Rapist" case is finally making decisive progress. Detective Constable Steve Irwin of the Toronto Metropolitan Police, who is in charge, is quickly certain that it is one man who committed all the rapes and attempted rapes. In addition, traces of semen can be recovered from the victims. In April 1992, the horrific series of rapes is brought to an end: Now, finally, the test results concerning the samples of suspects are available. Out of a total of 230 blood samples, only five match the blood factors of the rapist; one of them is Paul. Since the cultured, good-looking man does not fit the image of a serial rapist at all, the police are sorting him out again for the time being and are following the leads to the four other suspects. It will take ten more months before the forensic lab finally examines Paul Bernardo's DNA sample.

In the summer of 1992, domestic violence escalates at the Bernardos' home. Paul hits Karla in the head with a flashlight so hard that she has two black eyes and the most severe bruises. In early 1993, her parents manage to persuade her to seek shelter with her sister Lori when her husband is away on a business trip. But Karla drives back, insisting she has to get something important.

The police arrest Paul Bernardo after he beats his wife to hospital but release him for the time being. Shortly thereafter, Karla Homolka files for divorce from her husband.

In February 1993, both the Scarborough and Green Ribbon Task Force investigations gain momentum. With DNA results finally in, establishing that Paul Kenneth Bernardo is the rapist, the suspicion finally arises that both the acts in Scarborough, Bernardo's old residence, and the murders of the two teenagers at his new residence, St. Cathrines, may be related. Karla is intensively questioned by several police officers for five hours. She tactics skilfully: Following the interrogation, she confides in her uncle and confesses to him that Paul is both the "Scarborough rapist" and the killer of Leslie Mahaffy and Kristen French - then, she finds herself a good lawyer. Her choice falls on George Walker, whom Karla remembers from her days as a veterinary assistant. Back then, she cared for his cancer-stricken dog.

On February 17, 1993, Paul is arrested for two counts of murder. The next day, proceedings are opened against him in Scarborough for multiple counts of attempted and completed rape. The magistrate refuses to release him on bail.

Two days after the arrest, police secure a large amount of incriminating evidence during a search of the bungalow in Port Dalhousie. Paul Bernardo not only keeps detailed records of every single rape case in Scarborough; he also has an extensive library and video library on pornography of every kind, as well as fetishes. Furthermore, he collects literature and reports on serial killers. One of the videotapes found shows Karla having sex with two other women. Two days later, another videotape turns up - it is the footage of a rape. Investigators initially think the person recorded is Kristen French. Karla corrects the police officers and tells them it is the footage of her sister Tammy. She also admits that her sister did not die of natural causes, as was previously assumed. At this point, however, the police officers have no idea that there is more important evidence in the house.

On February 24, 1993, Karla Homolka is also arrested as an accomplice. She immediately agrees to testify against her 28-year-old ex-husband Paul. Her condition: She wants to receive a reduced sentence for her cooperation. The law enforcement authorities agree to this deal, so they have an important key witness. Just one day later, Karla's divorce from her husband Paul Bernardo is final.

Karla's lawyers and the prosecution negotiate fiercely. At issue are the specific terms in the leniency deal. A deal that will later turn out to be a pact with the devil. It assures Karla not only a short trial, but a maximum of 12 years in prison for each of the Mahaffy and French murders, with the time to be served concurrently. Furthermore, Homolka is assured the chance of parole after serving three years. She only has to plead guilty to two counts of manslaughter and testify fully and truthfully against her ex-husband. The blonde promptly agrees.

Her second attorney, Murray Segal, lobbies hard for Karla Homolka to be psychiatrically evaluated. During the psychiatric stay, which Karla immediately begins, she finally writes her parents a letter explaining the circumstances of Tammy's death and apologizing for everything. She doesn't want to lie any longer, she says. "He threatened me and abused me physically and mentally when I refused," the letter reads. Karla insists that she only did all this because Bernardo forced and pressured her. "There are no words that could make you understand what he did to me." Karla presents herself as another victim of Paul Bernardo.

On May 14, 1993, the State of Canada's previously negotiated plea deal with Karla Homolka finally becomes final. The report of her psychologist, Dr. Malcolm, is instrumental in ensuring that the plea bargain, which is extremely advantageous to Karla, actually comes to pass. He points out, "She "knew what was happening, but she felt completely helpless and unable to act in her own defense or the defense of others. She was, in my opinion, paralyzed with fear". For this reason, the psychologist suspects, Homolka simply obeyed. Also credited as positive are Karla Homolka's young age, lack of previous convictions, and the abuse she experienced at the hands of her husband, then issues the discussed verdict.

Karla Homolka only has to testify against her husband Paul Bernardo. The blonde also assists in reviewing the available video footage and helps investigators secure DNA traces of the victims in the Bernardos' bungalow. In addition, they find remnants of the cement, complete with a signed invoice, that Bernardo bought to bury Leslie Mahaffy's remains in.

One day after Karla Homolka agreed to the deal with the prosecution, on May 6, 1993, Paul Bernardo asks his lawyer Ken Murray to go to Port Dalhousie and get some hidden Super 8 film tapes from the bungalow. Although the lawyer gets a detailed description of the hiding place, it is still difficult for him to discover. However, he finally finds the tapes behind a light strip on the bathroom ceiling. Bernardo instructs him not to look at the recordings or tell anyone about them, but simply to keep the tapes until May 18, 1993. On that day, the verdict for Karla Homolka is to be announced.

The tapes are locked in a safe in the lawyer's office. On the day the verdict is announced, Ken Murray, following Bernardo's written instructions, looks at the tapes and makes copies, which he keeps in a safe place. The tapes show the rapes of Tammy Homolka, Leslie Mahaffy, Kristen French, as well as Jane Doe. Highly sensitive material, but Bernardo apparently wants to wait before bringing the videos into play. His lawyer agrees, although this is in stark contrast to the rules of his profession, and he is in an ethical dilemma with the favor. He withholds important evidence that incriminates his client, but on the other hand also exonerates him on certain points. His lawyer colleague John Rosen advises him to keep the videos under lock and key, saying that they are harmful in the current situation, but could become useful to possibly discredit Karla Homolka's testimony later.

Murray plans to use these videos as a basis to sue Karla after Bernardo's preliminary hearing to try to negotiate a plea for him or prove at trial that Bernardo did not kill Leslie Mahaffy and Kristen French, but Homolka did.

In August 1994, however, Bernardo's instructions changed. He now claims never to have had contact with the two victims and instructs Murray to make the videotapes disappear. Murray then resigns his commission and John Rosen takes over Bernardo's defense. Subsequently, Murray asks the Law Society for advice on what to do with the videotapes, and he receives a recommendation to turn them over to the Bernardo trial judge. He attempts to do so, however, with the court's approval, the tapes are turned over to John Rosen. The latter forwarded them to the police 12 days later. In all, Murray withholds the tapes for 17 months. He is charged with obstruction of justice but is ultimately acquitted.

It takes a full two years before Paul Bernardo's trial in relation to the crimes at St. Cathrines finally begins. Things only start to move again when Bernardo demands that his lawyer, Ken Murray, destroy the videotapes. However, these were an important element of his defense strategy, the tapes were to be used to substantiate that Karla was anything but a pitiful victim of her sadistic spouse, but rather an active, driving part. Paul had also relied on this variant up to this point, but after Karla got off so lightly, he prefers to claim that he didn't know Leslie Mahaffy and Kristen French at all, nor was he responsible for their deaths. Something that would be impossible to refute without the videos, he reasoned. At this point Murray resigns his mandate, in the future Paul Bernardo will be represented by John Rosen - and he does not hesitate for a moment and hands over the original videotapes to the police on September 22, 1994.

The first day of the trial against Paul Kenneth Bernardo is scheduled for May 18, 1995, in Toronto, Ontario. In this trial, he is charged with three counts of murder, aggravated assault, false imprisonment, kidnapping, and unworthy treatment of a corpse. The Scarborough trial is still ongoing concurrently. The reading of the indictment by prosecutor Ray Houlahan in Toronto takes a full day. In it, Houlahan describes Homolka's still assumed role as a victim in great detail. He even cites several videotapes as evidence, which shock those present in their permissiveness. Among other things, Homolka can be seen masturbating - while Bernardo gives her instructions as director. He is the "king," the footage says, and Karla plays his slave. On camera, she even promises to supply him with thirteen-year-old virgins. Only the jury gets to see the images; the trial observers only hear what was filmed - but this rivals any indexed porn film. Bernardo pleads not guilty, stating that Karla Homolka murdered the two girls. Bernardo's defense attorney, John Rosen, also manages to use the video scenes to sow doubt about the production of Karla Homolka, who presents herself as the innocent, tortured victim.

Karla Homolka also has an important date on May 18, 1995, as demands are still being made to hold her accountable for sexual assault, even though the actual trial against her has already ended. Specifically with regard to the acts against Jane Doe, it appears that the young woman may decide to face separate charges after all. The judge's decision during deliberations was that no further charges would be brought against Homolka in this regard; she had not denied such acts but could no longer remember anything due to post-traumatic stress disorder. She gets off scot-free due to alleged memory lapses. But is this the main reason why she is seen as a victim of Bernardo from the start rather than as an accomplice - or possibly even as the actual driving force?

Is this view of Karla Homolka perhaps simply based on a clichéd image of women, according to which women are gentle, caring, passive and motherly - unless they are threatened or blackmailed?

At the beginning of the investigations, such an impression suggests itself. From the beginning, Karla Homolka presents herself as a defenseless victim of Paul Bernardo - which his violent assault impressively underlines with visible injuries. She can thus position herself, without having to fear inquiries, as either a submissive person or as a person with signs of a dependent personality. The fact that she went to the bungalow in Port Dalhousie specifically to get something (which she could not find) before her arrest is not an issue at any point. But was she possibly looking for the videos that show Homolka's role in a significantly different light?

Far too quickly, she agrees to the deal that the prosecution offers her. Moreover, the woman obviously has no qualms about heavily incriminating her former dream man Paul Bernardo through her statements. For a long time, the rapist is considered the driving force behind the kidnappings and murders, but is he really? After all, Tammy, Jane Doe and Kristen French were fed to him by Karla Homolka, she provided the sleeping pills and anesthetics ...

But at the latest with the introduction of the videotapes as evidence, it also becomes clear that Karla Homolka was actively involved in the rapes and tortures and thus anything but a compliant victim. Moreover, it is her who insists that Leslie Mahaffy must die. She alone wants to have witnessed that the teenager's blindfold slipped, and that the girl thus might have had the opportunity to catch a glimpse of her tormentors.

Gradually, it becomes more and more obvious how skillfully this woman ultimately manipulated the government officials from the beginning. But in order to convict the alleged main perpetrator, Paul Bernardo, they were willing to use any means to get a prosecution witness who was willing to testify. This resulted in one of the worst legal deals ever made in a trial.

In one interrogation Paul Bernardo even repeatedly asks the police officers present why his ex-wife had never been subjected to a lie detector test until now? Then perhaps it would finally come out what she is hiding ...

The verdict in the case "The State of Canada v. Paul Bernardo" is handed down on September 1, 1995: The man, who was 31 years old at the time, is found guilty as charged and receives a life sentence. He is thus officially considered the main culprit in the kidnappings and murders of Leslie Mahaffy and Kristen French. Only after 25 years does he have the opportunity to apply for a pardon; but since he is considered highly dangerous and at high risk of recidivism, a pardon is relatively unlikely. On November 3 of the same year, Bernardo is also brought to justice by the Scarborough court for the acts of the Scarborough Rapist and the rape and death of Tammy Homolka. In this trial, he is also found guilty on all charges.

As of July 4, 2005, Karla Homolka, who also received multiple psychiatric evaluations during her time in custody and now calls herself Karla Teale, has been released after 12 years in prison. She did not apply for parole or early release during her time in prison and is serving her sentence to the last day, which is rather unusual for Canadian conditions. There is a tendency here to try to rehabilitate offenders as early as possible.

After her release in 2005, Karla Homolka, who now lives in Quebec, repeatedly receives anonymous death threats via a specially created Internet portal. Furthermore, the woman, who now calls herself Leanne Teale, is intensively observed and followed by the media. Press, radio and television are of the opinion that every Canadian has the right to know where the female part of the murderous "Ken-and-Barbie" duo is currently staying. The media emphasize that this is about protecting Canadian children.

Shortly after her release, Homolka marries her lawyer Sylvie Bordelais' brother, Thierry Bordelais, a native of the Caribbean. He is also the father of her first child, born in 2005.

In 2007, to escape media reenactments, the couple moves to their native Guadeloupe. However, Homolka, now calling herself Leanne Bordelais, is tracked down by the media here as well. The reporter sees Homolka, who has become thin, handling her now three children in the garden of her home, breastfeeding one of the children and preparing food for her family in an average kitchen. The surprising realization: "Barbie" Karla seems like a picture-perfect mother. She lovingly cares for her offspring, protects the children and makes sure that they have everything they need. The family does not have police protection, although a page was set up on the Internet where users bet on when someone would manage to track down and kill Karla Homolka.

In 2017, she is making news again: she lives in Canada again, in the middle-class Montreal suburb of Châteauguay. There, the former sex killer, who is still one of the most hated people in her homeland, is now involved in a local elementary school and leads what appears to be a completely normal life. The fact that Homolka occasionally accompanies the students on field trips causes regular agitation among the parents. On one occasion, she visits one of the primary school classes with her dog so that the children can learn how to get in touch with animals. All this caused a storm of indignation from the other parents.

In a CBS television interview recorded shortly after Homolka's release, she asks the anchor-woman, "Do you understand why people are so interested in you?" After glancing at her companion, Homolka replies with a smile, "Yes and no. Of course, I've done terrible things, there's no doubt about that. And it is also rare for a woman to do such things. On the other hand, there are, after all, many people released from prison every day who have also done terrible things." And she finally adds, after a pause, "I think I get it, though."

»50 murders per week on the screen are not an expression of additional freedom.«

- Egon Karl-Heinz Bahr (1922 -2015)
German politician-

CHAPTER 6

Bandit in make up

Guard George Hutchison can't help but yawn profusely as he goes on duty on the morning of September 9, 1952. His workplace is the disreputable Don Prison. Built in the 1860s, the building is located in Ontario's capital, Toronto. The prison, with its striking Italian-style facade, is named after the Don River, which meanders through the province to the east of the building. Hutchison wearily trudges through the corridor of the former hospital wing, which has since been converted into a cell block. The Don prison's conversion is owed to the increasing occupancy of the detention rooms by delinquents. Every time the warden passes one of the barred windows, the late warm summer sun's rays caress the man's face. On the way to his post, Hutchison muses about how it must feel for the inmates to have that little bit of the outside world they still get to see, day in and day out, viewed only through bars. While George is contemplating his thoughts, a sudden, disturbing discovery makes him feel wide awake. Four of the iron bars on one of the barred corridor windows have disappeared. A chill runs down the man's spine: "Please dear God, don't let this be true," the guard mutters to himself in a vain attempt to calm himself down. But a glance into the empty cells of the country's most notorious bank robbers leaves no doubt: along with the bars outside the window, the four prisoners have also disappeared without a trace. "Not again!" curses Hutchinson, before alerting his colleagues. The agitated guards search every nook and cranny of the detention center. As some of the guards rush into the detention center's courtyard and look around searchingly for the fugitives, they hear peals of laughter. The men turn and look up the façade of Don Prison. Hanging from one of the barred cell windows, an inmate glares down at them. "You fools, they're long gone!" he gleefully laughs at the guards.

...It is April 2, 1914, when Eleanor gives birth to her first son in Toronto. The little boy is just 4 months old when the British Empire, of which Canada is a member, declares war on Germany. In August 1915, father Glover joins the army and travels overseas to fight on the front lines in World War I. His son Edwin Alonzo is less than a year and a half old at the time. When the soldier returns home to his small family in 1919, it is as if a stranger moves in with his mother for Edwin, who is now 5 years old. He has no memory of his father, Glover Boyd. From then on, the religious veteran works as a security guard at the Toronto police station. Over the years, the Boyd couple has two more children. The growing family moves frequently. For the firstborn Edwin, who is called Eddie by everyone, the moves mean constant changes of school. But he has no trouble making friends with his classmates. The teenager impresses his friends by getting up to all kinds of mischief - regardless of the fact that his father is a policeman and has to ensure law and order.

...Eddie Boyd is 15 years old when his brothers Gord and Norm fall ill with the dreaded childhood disease scarlet fever. Mother Eleanor nurses the boys back to health. In the process, the woman contracts the bacterial infectious disease and dies as a result of the infection. The death of his mother throws the teenager off track.

He leaves school and runs away from home. As a stowaway, the boy travels on trains, along with other migrant workers called "hobos," through the western part of the country.

...The 1930s are marked by a severe economic crisis in the USA, which goes down in history as the "Great Depression". Eddie survives the dilemma despite all adversity. In the meantime, he has grown into an attractive young man and keeps his head above water with changing female acquaintances, poorly paid odd jobs and minor scams. Boyd is 22 years old when he goes too far: the young man robs a gas station. Eddie had already been arrested by the police for vagrancy, but this offense now earns him a two-and-a-half-year prison term.

...It is 1939 when the Second World War breaks out. Lacking other alternatives, the released criminal joins the military. In June 1940, his regiment sets out for France. Following the mission, the soldiers are called to the town of Reigate, located in the south of England. Eddie meets a girl here. Soon the couple marries, and Eddie adopts Doreen's son from a previous relationship. Only nine months after the wedding bells rang, Doreen gives birth to a baby boy on August 20, 1941. But just two days after the birth, a nurse drops the new-born from her arms during an air raid alert- the fall causes a brain hemorrhage and the infant, named after his father, dies.

...To be close to her husband during the war, the still grieving mother joins the ATS ("Auxiliary Territorial Service"). The ATS is the women's division of the British Army during World War II, whose members primarily perform support duties such as cooking, camp administration, and the like. Eddie, meanwhile, is increasingly fed up with military service. Ever since he was a teenager, the young man has hated rules of any kind. But the army's strict regulations make him think he can hardly draw a breath. And so it happens that the soldier with a criminal record is assigned to the military police, of all things. Only shortly after his transfer, Doreen is back in different circumstances. In December 1943, the young woman gives birth to healthy twins.

...Fourteen days after the end of World War II in Europe, Eddie Boyd receives his official discharge papers from the army. The couple returns to Canada from overseas with their three children. From then on, the family man works as a streetcar driver on the Yong Street line and part-time as a window cleaner. But Boyd soon grows bored with the disdainful rule-abiding civilian life. When Eddie hears a story about an autistic kid who allegedly robbed a bank without even using a gun, things start to work in the head of the handsome man with the dark eyes and square chin. "If it's that easy, why the hell am I spending my days working?", Eddie thinks to himself as he slips into his best suit. Then he squeezes some absorbent cotton and shoves it in his mouth to plump up his cheeks. Swiftly, the streetcar driver puts on some more makeup for further camouflage before reaching for a bottle to give himself courage. On September 9, 1949, Eddie commits his first bank robbery. When he returns to the scene a few days later, none of the employees recognize the robber. As a result, Boyd is sure of his infallibility. From now on, the hoodlum makes a living for his loved ones by robbing banks.

...In the coming weeks and months Eddie commits at least six bank robberies. Not infrequently, his crimes end with bullets whizzing around his ears, as bank employees are often equipped with revolvers to defend themselves and the money in the event of an attack. But the man always comes out of the hail of bullets unscathed. Boyd soon becomes notorious as the made-up robber who deftly leaps onto bank counters and deftly waves his German Luger pistol around in the air. He is not always alone in his crimes. At times he has accomplices and exactly one of them is to be his undoing. Howard Gault, who occasionally accompanies Boyd on his heists, walks right into the arms of the police after a botched robbery. After hours of interrogation, the robber breaks down and betrays his partner. After Boyd is arrested, he and Gault are sent to the notorious Don Prison in Toronto. The population, especially the bank employees among them, breathe a sigh of relief- finally the all-knowing robber is caught.

...In prison, Boyd meets Lennie Jackson, also convicted of bank robbery, who was imprisoned at about the same time as Eddie. The two felons, trapped together in a tiny cell, quickly make contact. Lennie's most striking feature is his wooden foot; the man had lost his own foot trying to jump onto a moving freight train.

...Pretty soon another bandit joins the duo: Willie Jackson, also known as "The Clown." The man, who is not related to Lennie, owes his nickname to his witty nature. Willie is in Don Prison awaiting transfer to Kingston Prison to serve a seven-year sentence for his numerous bank robberies.

...So it happens that Eddie; the handsome, the clown and the man with only one foot, make a plan together - they want to break out of the hated Don prison. Lennie's handicap proves to be a blessing for the bandits, for his prosthesis not only helps him to walk upright - the cunning man has also hidden a set of saw blades from the prison guards.

...On the night of Sunday, November 4, 1951, the three bank robbers saw off the bars of their cells and slide into the prison yard on a twelve-meter rope knotted from bed sheets. They scurry to the six-meter-high prison wall and climb to freedom. The coming weeks are to become a nerve-wracking test for the protective police officers, who are doing everything they can to apprehend the bandits again. Just two weeks have passed when the robbers again rob a bank in the west of Toronto and relieve it of 4300 dollars (equivalent to about 24,000 GBP today).

...Although the country's police officers are on high alert, the bandits manage to rob the Royal Bank in the Leaside neighborhood on November 20, 1951. Their loot amounts to 46,000 dollars (equivalent of about 250,000 GBP today). For the men, a lavish Christmas is now just around the corner. Eddie's wife Doreen and his three children spend the holiday in a motel on the western outskirts of Toronto. The wife later recalls Christmas Eve: "It was a real Christmas with presents and Christmas dinner-everything but a tree," the mother of three gushes.

...The "Clown," on the other hand, loses his laughter during the Christmas season of 1951. Willie Jackson meets a pretty woman in a Montreal tavern. The two flirt with each other and plenty of alcohol flows, which soon makes Jackson careless. To supposedly impress his counterpart, he flashes his loaded gun from the inside pocket of his jacket. To emphasize his boldness, he tells his new acquaintance that he has pulled off a spectacular escape from the dreaded Don prison. Thanks to the young woman's sense of duty, the police officers are able to catch the escapee.

...Even though there are suspicions that Lennie Jackson is the head of the gang, the newspapers prefer to name the criminals after the handsome, charming Eddie and christen the delinquents the "Boyd Gang". The men quickly find replacements for their arrested sidekick- henceforth, professional, but unsuccessful, violinist Steve Suchan joins Eddie and Lennie in the pursuit of quick riches. He was the one who gave shelter to the escapees and hid them from the guards, who left no stone unturned in search for the fugitives. In the meantime, the gang even hid their loot in Suchan's parents' house. His father offered the gangsters to keep the money in a small hiding place in the wall of the house. But the next morning, the old man and the money disappeared without a trace.

...Just a short time after the beginning of 1952, the gang strikes again - they rob a branch bank in Scarborough, an eastern suburb of Toronto. The men took 10,000 dollars (equivalent of about €48,000 GBP today). Just a few weeks later, the robbers are already plotting their next coup. It is March 4, 1952, when the "Boyd Gang" relieves a bank in Montreal of 2600 dollars (equivalent of about 14,500 GBP today).

...The police are feverishly searching for the bank robbers in order to give back the feeling of security to the population, as mostly shocked customers are inside the banks, while the "Boyd Gang" are shouting and threatening the employees. During their series of robberies, the men capture about $75,000 (equivalent of about 420,000 GBP). Just two days after the latest robbery, police officers Edmund Tong and Roy Perry are patrolling the West End when they wave out a car to make a routine check on the two male occupants. As Tong approaches the black Mercury Monarch, he is unaware of the danger he is in until the driver of the car knocks him to the ground with a shot from the window. Badly wounded, the policeman collapses. His colleague Perry, who is still sitting in the police car, is the target of the shooter. Quick-witted, the policeman holds his arm in front of his face, is wounded but prevents a bullet from hitting him in the head. The Mercury's wheels roll, and the gunman and his companion flee. Edmund Tong is taken to a hospital and succumbs to his severe gunshot wounds a few days later - but not before he can inform his colleagues that none other than Steve Suchan is his murderer and Lennie Jackson his accomplice.

...The death of the policeman pushes his colleagues to catch the members of the "Boyd gang" and bring them to justice. Although Eddie Boyd was not involved in the shooting, the incident ensures that the newspapers print his portrait on every front page. While Eddie and Doreen had at least been able to leave their house under cover of darkness until then, the couple is now deprived of even that little bit of freedom. From now on they have to stay hidden.

...In the meantime, the police are working at full speed. Not thirty hours after their colleague Tong was fatally injured, the investigators break into Suchan's apartment and wait for the killer to return. Sure enough, the unsuspecting tenant soon enters his home. "Police! Freeze!" the uninvited guests yell at him. Steve reaches for his holster, which contains his revolver. But before he can reach for the gun, one of the police officers shoots the man. The bullet just misses Steve's heart.

...A few days later, the lawmen also track down Lennie Jackson. After a neighbor of the wanted man tells the policemen where the robber lives, the police take up position in Jackson's apartment and wait for the man's return. Unlike Suchan, the capture of Lennie does not go smoothly at all. The robber opens fire on the lawmen before they can react. One of the cops hastily fires a shot before fleeing with his colleagues, slamming the apartment door behind him. A protracted exchange of gunfire through the closed door ensues. Some 200 bullets whiz through the air in 45 minutes on that March 11, 1952, until the cops hear the wounded Jackson shout from inside the apartment: "I quit!". Only with tear gas bombs that burn Lennie's eyes and lungs do the protective guards manage to apprehend the man. Jackson, like Suchan, ends up in a hospital. Both gangsters survive their arrests and face murder charges.

...Investigators are also able to quickly locate Eddie Boyd's hideout. He is hiding out, along with his wife and one of his brothers, in a rented apartment. The legendary detective Adolphus Payne decides to wait for the dawn of the coming day before arresting the gangster. At any cost, he wants to prevent another shooting. And so, Payne, together with his partner, sneaks into Boyd's hideout on March 15, 1952. He stalks, gun drawn, to the bedside of the hunted man, who snoozes there peacefully beside his wife, Doreen. In front of the bed, the officer discovers a bag filled with guns and $25,000 (equivalent of about 175,000 GBP today). Adolphus holds the gun to the sleeping Boyd's forehead and yells, " This is Payne! Give up already!". And indeed, the arrest of Eddie proceeds without an exchange of gunfire and without resistance from the criminal.

...Boyd returns to the most desolate place imaginable. His joy is all the greater when one day his crony Willie, as well as Lennie and Suchan, reappear at Don Prison. Both have recovered from their injuries in the hospital. The prison management, probably without giving much thought, had decided to house the "Boyd gang" in the otherwise empty death row wing. Weeks and months pass, giving the men time to meticulously plan their next escape. Although the guards have removed Lennie Jackson's prosthetic foot, forcing the man to use a tin can lined with a sock as a substitute, this chicanery does nothing to change the gang's ingenuity.

...They manage to bribe someone to smuggle a piece of metal, a file and saw blades into the prison. After making mock friends with one of the older guards, they fool around with him one day. One of the gang members, as if to joke, grabs the key ring attached to the guard's belt. Firmly, he squeezes the cell key, which can open all four of the gangsters' detention rooms, in his hand. And sure enough, a perfectly fitting imprint appears in the palm of his hand. Using the smuggled-in tools, the prisoners make a duplicate key. As soon as the guards are out of sight, the criminals take turns freeing themselves from their cells and, in every unobserved minute, sawing unnoticed at one of the window bars in the corridor until sparks fly. To make it easier to squeeze through the sawn hole between the bars, the men each shed about 9 kilograms. "It was the hardest time of my life," William Jackson later reports. "But the best reason to be on a diet I've ever heard of," "The Clown" adds in a quip. None of the guards seem to notice that the gangsters are slimming down and leaving most of their meals on their plates. "But you can't blame the guards," Eddie Boyd recounts with a sly grin on his face, "a lot of people at the Don just can't stand the food."

...Before the morning of Sept. 8, 1952, dawns, the prisoners squeeze through the painstakingly sawed hole in the window grate and crawl along the prison wall at a lofty height before taking the plunge to the ground and immediately running down a hill to their freedom. Their crony Lennie, who can only move with a limp without his prosthetic foot, is supported by the gangsters and thus also helps him to escape from the Don prison. The men, also with the help of friendly hoodlums living in freedom, have planned their escape in detail. On the way to their hideout, one of the "Boyd gang" buddies has deposited a prosthetic foot. After Lennie slips his stump into the wooden foot, the men make their way to an abandoned barn 24 kilometers from the prison. Here they plan to hold out until the population loses interest in the fugitives. The men's only belongings are three guns, 96 bullets, $50 (equivalent of about 430 GBP today) and a razor. Who got them all these things, the gangsters will never reveal?

...William Jackson uses the razor to disguise himself. He shaves a bald spot across the base of his forehead and sets out to shop at a grocery store, located on a busy street. In fact, no one recognizes the man and this despite the fact that the authorities have offered an almost unbelievably high reward, for clues leading to the capture of the gang, in the amount of 26 000 dollars (equivalent of about 180,000 GBP today). Nevertheless, the fugitive gangsters are not infrequently spotted; however, most witnesses think the men are just migrant workers seeking shelter in the abandoned barn. Nevertheless, some observers soon become suspicious and alert the police. The lawmen, armed to the teeth, have been searching for the fugitive hoodlums for days. They combed every corner of the city and all known places of the underworld.

...It is September 16, 1952, when an armada of heavily armed police surround the barn. Seeing the hopeless situation, the "Boyd Gang" surrenders without offering any resistance and the escapees are shipped back to Don Prison.

...A few weeks later, the men are put on trial. Edwin Alonzo Boyd receives several life sentences for several bank robberies and lesser offenses. His crony Willie Jackson gets a sentence of 31 years. Lennie Jackson and Steve Suchan are sentenced to death for the murder of police officer Edmund Tong. But not only the members of the "Boyd gang" get punishments: also all to be found contributors to the escapes of the delinquents receive sanctioning.

...On December 16, 1952, Suchan climbs onto the execution platform, Lennie hops after him; the man is not allowed to wear his prosthetic foot when he dies. Back to back, the condemned stand on the trapdoor set into the floor as the executioner slips a canvas sack over their heads and places a thickly knotted noose around their necks. Then he routinely pulls the lever and the two criminals plunge to their deaths.

...The imprisonment of the well-known robber is a drastic experience for his wife Doreen and their three children. Now a single parent, she initially has difficulty finding work to support her family. And social contempt also hits Boyd's offspring especially hard. Daughter Carolyn recalls, "It was hard not having a father, but it was harder to deal with the consequences. For example, most parents wouldn't let their kids play with us. The kids called us jailbirds and accused us of stealing."

...In 1966, Willie Jackson is released on parole. The man henceforth pursues honest employment as a janitor. The same year as Jackson, authorities also grant Eddie parole. Boyd divorces Dorren assumes a new identity and moves to British Columbia. Eddie, too, now earns his money with honest work: he drives a bus that transports people with handicaps. Here he meets his second wife and cares for her for the next 35 years, until institutionalization can no longer be averted.

...On May 17, 2002, Canada's most notorious bank robber dies at the age of 88 as a result of pneumonia. It is 2011 when movie director Nathan Morlando, in cooperation with Boyd's daughter Carolyn, processes the life of the charismatic criminal in the drama "Gangsters". But the director recounts, "It was very easy for Boyd to turn on his charm, point his finger as if it were a gun, and say he didn't regret robbing the bank. But when I caught him in a quieter moment, I could see deep regret in his eyes. He was heartbroken at the loss of his family and children." Boyd's offspring continue to endure the loss of their beloved father to incarceration and his gangster image glorified by the media into adulthood. In particular, the visits of the incarcerated head of the family to the prison with the large, heavy doors, are gruesomely remembered by the adult daughter Carolyn. Morlando's work reveals the mental pain the charismatic bandit inflicted on his family with his actions. "When the film was finished, I said (...) that this would be the end. There will be no 'Rocky II.' It's over," Carolyn relates with relief.

If you read the story of a great criminal make sure that before you condemn them you always thank the good heavens for not putting your honest face at the beginning of such a series of circumstances.

- Georg Christoph Lichtenberg (1742 – 1799)
Founder of the German-language aphorism. -

CHAPTER 7

The Mask

(by Sarah Fischer / Eyes in the Dark - the Podcast)

Friday at last - the calendar shows October 10, 2008, the day John Altinger will meet his Internet acquaintance Jen for the very first time. The two have been exchanging messages for a while now and John has a good feeling about her. Euphorically, he tells some of his closest friends about the planned date with his supposed dream girl. He lives only a few minutes' drive from the agreed meeting place, but nevertheless he sets off on time for Jen's apartment that evening. Jen lives in the southern part of Edmonton, the capital of the Canadian province of Alberta - a good neighborhood.

Although John had assured his friends that he would hear from them after the date, he doesn't get in touch at first. The queasy feeling that spreads among John's friends, however, is drowned out by the hope that the date went particularly well. Johnny will get back to them when he has time, he always has. They were to be proved right: Three days after the meeting, John contacts his best friend by e-mail, in which he raves about his new acquaintance. The two had spontaneously decided to visit Jen's winter home in Costa Rica to spend the next weeks together. He would not be back in town before December 10, 2008. But he would check his e-mails regularly and send a phone number to his friends. He ends his email with a snappy "See you at the holidays. Johnny." This message strikes a bitter chord with John's friends; it doesn't sit well with the 38-year-old at all. It's all happening way too fast. But when John quits his job a few days later, also via e-mail, the alarm bells start ringing in his circle of acquaintances. This is not the John they knew. Promptly, some of his friends decide to go to John's apartment to check up on him. On the spot, they immediately notice that his car is not there. Moreover, his two motorcycles are not covered with a tarp as usual. The motorcycles are John's babies; under no circumstances would he leave them like that. Finally, they had had enough. But upon arriving at the police station, the police officers explain to them that these clues are not sufficient for a missing person report - there is no reasonable suspicion for a violent crime. Moreover, John is communicating with the outside world.

Sobered, but still determined to find John, his friends once again make their way to the small apartment where the man lives. They gain unauthorized access to his apartment and discover something that makes their blood run cold: Johnny's passport is on the dining room table. How could John have flown to Costa Rica if he didn't have his passport with him? Except for John's laptop, everything is in place. John would never have traveled without luggage. Armed with this knowledge, they head back to the police headquarters. At this point, the local police take the young men's concerns seriously and begin an investigation. The first thing they have to do is find this "Jen" whom John Altinger had met a few days ago on the dating platform "Plenty of fish".

The first useful clue that the police follow up comes from John's Internet acquaintance herself. In one of the e-mails exchanged, Jen had sent him detailed directions to her house - and John Altinger had taken the precaution of forwarding this e-mail to one of his best friends. Bingo! Less than an hour later, investigators are standing in front of a rundown two-car garage, in a nondescript back alley in south Edmonton. Mark Twitchell, a local producer and filmmaker, has rented this garage and uses it mostly as a movie studio. When the police contact him, he immediately makes his way to his garage to allow investigators access. He is an unassuming, tall man with a penchant for science fiction, fantasy films and well-made thrillers. A creative mind who has had the dream of becoming a successful film producer since his youth. When he's not honing his film career, he spends his free time with his newlywed wife and their daughter. The little girl is less than a year old.

Arriving at the detached double garage, Mark immediately notices a padlock - which he had not put there. Upon entering the garage, he notices other discrepancies: Several items are no longer in their original places, including a roll of duct tape, several trash bags, paper towels and a trash can. Mark and his crew had just finished filming a script he had written in the garage. An 8-minute thriller called "House of Cards", inspired by the TV series "Dexter". Since the filming had dragged on into the late evening hours, he decided not to return to the garage until a few days later. According to his own statements, he cleaned up the mess they had made during the shoot as planned on the second weekend of October. After that, he only went back once to unload newly procured cleaning supplies. Apart from him, however, two of his closer friends would also have a key to the garage he had rented. However, neither his friends nor himself knew a woman named Jen. While investigators look around the garage, they don't notice anything suspicious besides various film paraphernalia and some fake blood residue from the shoot. "Maybe John Altinger was out of town after all?" the cops ponder. But a check of the flight records from the last few days proves the opposite: John Altinger could not possibly have left the country on a plane. The investigators are in the dark. Surely the man could not have vanished into thin air.

The only clue the investigators have is the directions to Mark Twitchell's garage. Did they miss something back there? As Mark has been very cooperative, the police once again make contact with the film producer. As expected, Mark agrees to another search of his garage and hands the keys over to the investigators. The young man also takes this opportunity to share some details with the investigators that he had considered trivial during his first questioning. Mark tells that in the last few days - besides the strange padlock - there have been other strange incidents. Among other things, various personal items have been stolen during a break-in at his car. In addition, he and his wife Jess have the suspicion that, during a Thanksgiving party at her parents, a strange person must have been in their house. For when they come home, the front door is unlocked. But they properly locked the door when they left. They are sure of that. On top of that, during this conversation Mark reconstructs an encounter with a man that took place on October 15, 2008: As Mark is standing at a gas station and sitting in his car, a man unknown to him suddenly knocks on his window. The man, who also introduces himself as Mark, talks about his encounter with a well-off woman and an upcoming, extensive vacation that the two have planned. Since his new acquaintance wants to buy him a new car after the vacation, he would like to sell his old car as soon as possible. Since Mark is not in such a good financial position at the moment, he dug out his wallet and waved his last 40 dollars (about 30 GBP). Against his expectations, the stranger replied "Sold!", which means Mark is now the proud owner of a red Mazda.

This story makes the investigators suspicious. "Who sells their car for $40?" the officers wonder. They immediately check to see who the car's registered owner is. The investigators' uneasy gut feeling is quickly confirmed: the rightful owner of the newly acquired car is the missing John Altinger. Reason enough for another official interview with Mark Twitchell. Asked about this encounter, Mark becomes more and more entangled in contradictions. The investigators are sure: either Mark himself is responsible for the disappearance of John Altinger or he knows more than he admits. To get to the bottom of this suspicion, they confiscate Mark's car and order a large-scale search of his house and rented garage. They focus on all electronic devices - Mark's computer, his cameras, external hard drives and his film footage. Driven by the suspicion that John could be on one of the videos. But no evidence is found. During the search of his car, some handwritten notes attract the investigators' attention: one of the notes contains detailed directions to two different locations - one leads to the house of Mark Twitchell's first girlfriend, the other to the building complex where John Altinger lives. But that's not everything: among several small notes and junk, the investigators come across a bloody hunting knife. On top of that, they discover a large stain in the trunk of the car that looks like dried blood. They also find a black field hockey mask that appears to be covered in blood spatters. What happened here?

A document with the file name "SKConfessions" that the police officers find on Mark Twitchell's laptop provides information about this. The investigators can't believe their eyes when they restore the temporarily deleted file and go through it step by step. The 42-page document opens with the following paragraph: "This story is based on true events. The names and events have been slightly changed to protect the guilty party. This is the story of my progression to serial killer. Like anyone learning a new skill, I had to try things out and make mistakes at the beginning of my journey. Allow me to start from the beginning and I think you will see what I mean. I don't remember the exact place and time when I decided to become a serial killer, but I do remember the feeling that came over me when I made that decision. It was a rush of pure euphoria." The investigators are taken aback and ponder, "Is this a written confession?" But after just a few pages, lead investigator Mike Stabler catches his breath - according to the script, the author's first victim managed to escape his tormentor. This could be the breakthrough in the case. They need to track down this stranger. No sooner said than done.

Just a few hours later, Stabler, an experienced criminalist, stands in front of a dozen journalists and holds up the field hockey mask with a gold stripe found on Mark Twitchell to the cameras. A black field hockey mask with a golden stripe. The wanted unknown person should recognize the masking. According to the script, the perpetrator wore it during the attack. It must have burned itself into his victim's mind. And sure enough, as Gilles Tetreault thoughtlessly scrolls through his Facebook home page, he comes across an article featuring the black and gold field hockey mask. He freezes, but Tetreault knows exactly what to do. The man immediately reports to the police and that same day goes to the local police station for questioning and describes his encounter with the stranger, who was wearing a distinctive field hockey mask: On October 03, 2008, Gilles follows directions to a two-car garage in Edmonton. There he is supposed to meet his Internet acquaintance Sheena, with whom he has already been communicating for several days via the dating platform "Plenty of fish". As agreed, he crawls through the small slit of the gate to get into the garage. A few seconds after entering, Gilles suddenly feels someone grab him from behind and mace him with a stun gun. A moment of sheer panic. Gilles turns around and finds himself face to face with a man wearing a black and gold field hockey mask. At that moment, he realizes that this is not a rendezvous. The masked man pulls out a gun, orders Gilles to kneel on the ground and tapes his eyes shut. As Gilles lies on the ground, he realizes, "If I'm going to die, I'd rather die my way than his way." Determined not to give up without a fight, he stands up, rips the tape from his eyes and reaches for his attacker's gun.

Instantly, Tetreault realizes the gun is plastic. This is his chance to fight for his life: a fierce scuffle breaks out, which Gilles uses in his favor. With each blow of the attacker, he staggers a little further towards the garage door. Therefore, he allows the blows to continue until he is close enough to the gate to crawl through. His adversary grabs him by the collar in a last desperate attempt - but to no avail. Gilles deftly wriggles out of his jacket and escapes. But the man doesn't get far - just outside the garage door he feels the effects of the stun gun. His legs give out and Gilles collapses. Now he's struggling on all fours through the dirt when he suddenly notices his attacker coming up behind him again and grabs him by the ankles. "If I don't function now, that's it," Gilles thinks to himself. For a split second, the attacker loses his grip. The adrenaline rush Gilles desperately needed to survive floods his body. In a flash, he picks himself up and runs onto the small sidewalk that had previously led him to the garage. There he collapses again, right at the feet of a young couple - his salvation. The young couple can hardly believe their eyes when they spot the masked man close behind Gilles. Promptly, the latter calls out, "Buddy, come back." - "Is this show part of an elaborate robbery?" the couple thinks to themselves, so they make a hasty getaway.

The masked man, presumably due to the potential witnesses, lets go of Gilles and disappears into his garage. Gilles manages to get into his car and drives away. Once home, he checks his message history with "Sheena," but his Internet acquaintance's profile already no longer exists. Out of shame, he decides to keep quiet. Until that day. While Gilles recounts his experience with the masked man, the investigators can only shake their heads. Because what Gilles Tetreault tells them, drenched in sweat, exactly coincides with the manuscript they discovered on Mark Twitchell's laptop. That can't be a coincidence. But the script does not prove Mark's guilt either. Gilles Tetreault has not seen the face of his attacker and therefore cannot identify him. Mark Twitchell insists that the manuscript is merely a fictional script for one of his thrillers. Although investigators are now certain that Mark is the perpetrator, he remains at large. The circumstantial evidence gathered so far is not sufficient for an indictment. For this reason, Mark Twitchell is also able to get up in a good mood on the morning of October 31, 2008 and leave for an important meeting with a potential investor.

"Halloween, a good sign," Mark thinks to himself. After all, it's his favorite day of the year. He still longs for his big breakthrough in the film industry and is finally one big step closer to it - or so he thinks. But that hope is dashed when a special tactical unit storms out of a box truck and handcuffs Mark, who is on his way to a meeting. Twitchell is arrested for the murder of John Altinger and charged the same day. With the forensic analysis of the samples from his car, investigators have been able to gather enough incriminating evidence after all. Nevertheless, Mark stands by his original statement: he had nothing to do with John's disappearance. The investigators are dependent on a confession, because they cannot prove that he committed the crime. Among other things, one of the most important pieces of evidence is still missing: John's body has still not been found. Trials without finding a body do happen; however, the success for a conviction is much lower. He admits to the accusations made by Gilles Tetreault, but says it was just a PR stunt for his next project. After all, nothing more happened to Gilles. Apart from that, Mark Twitchell does not make any further statements about the accusations.

This attitude only changes in June 2010: Mark wants to talk to the investigators. But when he stands before Mike Stabler again almost a year and a half later, the man cannot utter a word and silently hands the murder investigator a folded piece of paper. On the front is a printed Google Maps map including detailed directions to a very specific location - "The Deposition Site of John Altinger's Remains" is written in block letters above it. As described in the manuscript, Mark Twichtell's directions lead to a manhole cover. Last year, the police had already searched several sewers on the basis of the descriptions in the document - but without success. Until today.

Not even a block away from the suspect's parents, the officers open one of the manhole covers they did not examine last year. And they find what they are looking for: The long and nerve-wracking search for John Altinger has come to an end-investigators recover the young man's remains in the underground sewer. When the first-degree murder trial of Mark Twitchell begins in 2011, the document titled "SKConfessions" is one of the most important pieces of evidence. Not only does this script realistically depict the failed, first trial; the author also details the successful second trial. The hair-trigger description of the approach, the murder and the subsequent disposal of the body, coincides with the evidence collected by the investigators.

On the second day of the trial, the 42-page letter is read and traces the final hours of John Altinger's life: John Altinger meets a young woman named "Jen" on the dating platform, whom he plans to finally meet outside the chat room on October 10, 2008. At this point, John has no idea that he is not in for a romantic first date, but that he has taken the bait laid out by Mark Twitchell. Hoping for the best, he sets off for his date - a little earlier than agreed. Jen had only sent him directions; she didn't want to give him an exact address for the time being. When John Altinger pulls up in front of the two-car garage, Mark Twitchell is already in his self-proclaimed "kill room," ready not to screw up again this time. His garage is still fixed up from the first, failed attempt; this time, everything is supposed to go like clockwork. But suddenly a dark male voice calls out, "Hello?" - John is early. Mark Twitchell knows John must have already seen his feet-he knows someone is there. But he is prepared for this: In the messages to John, "Jen" had already mentioned a man who occasionally uses the garage on weekends to do a workshop there. "Hi, I'm Harry" Mark replies triumphantly, "Jen is running about 20 minutes late. Would you like to wait here or come back?" John decides to leave. Mark tries to get ready during this time. Today is the day. Today he had to go through with it. But even when John Altinger pulls up in front of the garage again a good 20 minutes later, Mark Twitchell is still not ready. John's early appearance has completely thrown him off his game. John decides to leave a second time. This time to his home. Once there, John sits down at his desk and opens the dating platform "Plenty of fish" again. He struggles a bit, yet eventually still gets up the nerve to compose a message to Jen. Shortly after, a reply from Jen lights up and just a few minutes later, John is back in his red Mazda on his way to meet his Internet acquaintance. Unsuspecting that Mark Twitchell is waiting in his garage, ready to take advantage of the element of surprise. As John again crawls under the garage door, he tells Harry "I guess I'm just a fan of punishment." "You have no idea," Mark retorts, hitting him in the back of the head with an iron bar. Several times. There is no turning back now. A fight for life and death begins. Now he must put an end to it all, Mark thinks to himself. He pulls out the hunting knife that the investigators would later seize in his car and stabs him. He leaves John Altinger to bleed out next to the plastic sheets originally intended for the purpose. That part of his plan didn't work, the blood spills from the tarps onto the floor. Now he needs to get rid of the body. First things first: First, he cuts open John Altinger's pants and throws them into the big steel barrel he got just for that purpose. This is followed by John's top. After he has stripped the dead man as far as possible, he begins to carefully dismember his body. He had deliberately chosen his tools for this moment. The knife glides through the flesh as if it were nothing. It hardly bleeds at all. No wonder, after all, much of the blood was already spread across the garage floor. Contrary to Mark's expectations, cutting up a human body was anything but exciting. To make the process a little more amusing for himself, he sings as he does it, talks to himself, and thinks about tools he could get for dismembering his next victim.

After neatly placing the dismembered body in plastic bags, he removes the bloodstains and fingerprints in the garage with pure ammonia. He spends the following days with his wife Jess and their daughter. After all, it's Thanksgiving. But on Sunday morning, he has to get back to more important things. First, Mark Twitchell makes his way to his victim's apartment. Once there, he gains access to the small apartment to cover his tracks: He deletes John's dating profile and without further ado decides to take his victim's laptop. He plans to make the device disappear. Next, he has to dispose of John's body. Arriving at his "kill room," Mark Twitchell maneuvers the plastic bags filled with John's remains into his car. With the body parts in the trunk, he soon arrives at his parents' home, where he fails in his attempt to burn John's remains in a large steel barrel. Despite a considerable amount of gasoline and an even larger jet flame, burning the human body proves more difficult than suspected. Suddenly Mark hears police sirens and panics. He puts out the fire and thinks of a more effective way to get rid of the body. Ultimately, he decides to dump the remains in the manhole he marks on the printed Google Maps map two years later to lead investigators to John's body. Finished.

After the prosecutor reads the final sentences of the manuscript, a stifling silence spreads through the courtroom. In a last attempt to save himself, Mark Twitchell answers the charges - that he acted in self-defense. John Altinger had attacked him, he *had to* defend himself. The "SKConfessions" document he wrote would be based on this encounter but would have been embellished and changed by him afterwards.

The claim that the attack on John was meant to be a PR stunt that went awry is not believed by the convened jury. The descriptions written down in the manuscript are too gruesome and macabre. But in addition to the written description of the crime, the prosecution presents further serious evidence that speaks against the defendant: The blood residue found in Mark's car is proven to have come from the man who was killed. The hunting knife found in Mark's car had DNA traces of John Altinger, making it highly likely to be the murder weapon. Forensic experts were able to use the blood identifier Luminol to make large bloodstains visible under black light, which had previously been removed from Mark Twitchell's rented garage. In the course of the trial, the young film producer's suspected motive repeatedly flashed up: Mark Twitchell's obsessive interest in the television series "Dexter". Various fan pages he subscribed to and a Facebook profile he created for this purpose illustrate Mark Twitchell's personal identification with the main character Dexter Morgan, a vigilante serial killer. The press therefore christened the defendant the "Dexter Killer."

On April 12, 2011, Mark Twitchell aka the "Dexter Killer" is found guilty of the first-degree murder of John Altinger and sentenced to life in prison. He will not be eligible for parole for at least 25 years. For the killer, this means he cannot apply for early release until 2036. At present, the convict is serving his sentence in a correctional facility in Saskatchewan, Canada, passing the time with his self-acquired television set. In the meantime, he has caught up on every "Dexter" episode he has missed since his conviction.

I am a barbarian because I am not understood by anyone.

- Ovid (43 BC - 17 AD)
ancient roman poet-

CHAPTER 8

Bus 1170

(by Laura Regenauer / Eyes in the Dark - the Podcast)

It's July 30, 2008, when 22-year-old Tim McLean boards the Greyhound bus bound for Winnipeg. It's warm and stuffy on this bus, but that doesn't bother Tim in the least - he's used to long bus journeys and the circumstances that come with them. He chooses the second-to-last row on the right-hand side as his seat. There he sits down by the window so that he can at least get a little sleep during the journey. He will need some rest, as the trip from Edmonton to Winnipeg covers a distance of over 1,300 km and takes around 24 hours, including a few breaks. But even with the length of the trip Tim has no problems, the anticipation of seeing his family and friends again prevails quite clearly. In addition, during such a bus trip, one can get to know many and above all interesting people.

Around 6 p.m. bus 1170 reaches another stop on the list: Erickson in Manitoba. At this point, the bus trip has already lasted Tim 18 long hours. New passengers keep boarding the bus, and Erickson is no exception. The newly boarded passenger wears sunglasses on his nose and a black T-shirt, despite the late hour. Unlike Tim, he chooses a seat at the front of the bus. He remains seated there quietly and looks out through the window until a break is taken in Brandon at 7:00 pm. The bus stops there a little longer than at previous stops to give passengers a chance to stretch their legs a bit and fortify themselves with a meal for the onward journey.

By 7:30 p.m., the break is over, and the ride continues, with Tim back in his previous seat by the window. The guest who boarded in Erickson, Vincent Li, on the other hand, decides to change his seat. He starts walking slowly through the bus looking around, Tim looks up at him and says "Hi, how are you?". Shortly after, 40-year-old Vincent decides to take the seat next to Tim. By the time he does, his new seatmate is fast asleep again.

The bus rolls quietly along the highway, it is dark inside. The only light is that of the television, which is currently showing the movie "The Mask of Zorro". In the row directly opposite Tim and Vincent sits a couple, who periodically cast a glance in the direction of the two men. They see Vincent holding a toilet paper roll in one hand and a bottle of iced tea in the other. As soon as he takes a sip of iced tea, he clamps the toilet paper roll between his chin and chest. He then takes it back in his hand. They also observe Vincent rocking back and forth in his seat from 8:00 p.m. while mumbling something under his breath. What exactly the man says, however, the two do not understand, because it is a language unknown to them.

Around 9:00 p.m., the bus is 10 kilometers away from Portage La Prarie. Only 45 minutes to go until Tim reaches his long-awaited destination of Winnipeg; his home. He grew up near Winnipeg on a farm in Eli. Tim is a very adventurous boy from early on, whose dream has always been to travel. Sitting still is definitely not one of his strengths, quite the opposite - the more action the better. He is constantly on the lookout for new ventures and adventures.

What is very useful for him is his open and cordial nature - he quickly gets into conversation with strangers and has no problems to make new contacts everywhere.

In the summer of 2007, his cell phone rings, and on the other end of the line is Tiffany, one of Tim's close friends. She knows him well, so she knows how spontaneous he is. So, she asks him if he already has something planned for the summer - Tim says he doesn't. She didn't expect any other answer. Then nothing else stands in the way of their plan - she tells Tim to pack his things, at least for a week, but they will probably be on the road for longer.

Together they look for a job as carnies at a fair that travels all over the country. They can't imagine a better summer, a great job, cool people, and even traveling - for them, this appears to be the jackpot. Their expectations are not only met, but even exceeded. The whole team is like one big family; they work during the day and then party the heck out of it in the evening. In fact, they like it so much that they decide to extend their jobs for another year. The money is another plus; sometimes they make $1,000 a week per person. However, saving money doesn't cross their minds, this year is all about enjoying their young lives and celebrating properly.

During his travels, Tim films as much as he can to give his friends and family an insight into his world. His favorite means of transportation has always been the bus - not only because of the low prices, but mainly because it gives him the opportunity to meet new people. Tim is not someone who values luxury when traveling - the fun and experiences are his main focus.

The next stop of the fair, where Tim and Tiffany work, is Regina, following the city of Edmonton. But in Regina things have to go on without Tim from now on - because he is on his way home. At home in Winnipeg, he wants to do some things - to take care of his move as soon as possible. Tim wants to settle down in British Columbia, meet a woman there and start a family. To take care of everything that needs to be taken care of Tim plans to spend a week at home. To make the trip a little easier for him, his showman colleagues offer to put money together for him to buy him a plane ticket. But Tim declines with gratitude and buys a bus ticket instead.

It is July 30, 2008. Shortly after 9:00 p.m., the 1170 bus is filled with bloodcurdling screams. They are the screams of 22-year-old Tim McLean. Vincent Li is bent over him, stabbing the young man again and again. The passenger, who is sitting in the same row on the other side of the bus, yells to the bus driver to stop - but they are still in the middle of the Trans Canada Highway, making it harder for the bus driver to find a suitable place to stop.

Meanwhile, Tim tries to escape from his attacker by climbing over him. But in doing so, he falls back to the ground and Vincent has the opportunity to continue stabbing him. Like a robot, without emotions. There is no anger in his gaze, no aggression.

The bus manages to stop, and people flee outside in panic. 3 of the total 37 passengers were sitting behind Tim and his attacker, making it impossible for them to escape in the first moment. The passenger who alerted the bus driver of the attack goes back once more to help those three. Together they manage to get out of the bus unharmed. From the outside, the passengers can now watch in horror what is happening inside the bus. Vincent Li stabs his defenseless victim a total of 40-50 times until Tim stops moving. But apparently this is not enough for the attacker, as the horror continues.

With his large hunting knife in his hand, the perpetrator begins to sever Tim's head from his body. Now he holds the knife in one hand and the severed head in the other. Slowly he walks up and down the aisle in the middle of the bus. Suddenly, he turns to the window with his head in his hand and holds it up so that his fellow passengers can see him clearly.

A truck driver is also driving along this route that day until he suddenly spots the bus on the side of the road. He observes the panicked people and suspects that something terrible is going on there. Shortly after, he is confirmed in his assumption - because one of the passengers standing at the side of the bus calls out to him that they urgently need help; that a man has just been killed here. The truck driver doesn't hesitate for long, but stops, grabs a large metal pole from his car and slowly moves towards the bus.

The plan is to confront the attacker directly at first, and so the truck driver makes his way to the bus. However, when he sees exactly what the attacker has done to Tim's body, he no longer thinks confrontation is the best idea. Instead, they try to prevent the man from escaping and 3 men brace themselves against the door. For a short time, they look Vincent Li in the eyes, his gaze blank, completely devoid of emotion. It almost seems as if he doesn't even know what he has just done.

When Vincent realizes that he can't leave the bus through the door, he tries to start the bus to drive away with it. But fortunately, the bus driver had taken appropriate precautions by activating the immobilizer, and so this escape attempt also fails.

More and more police officers appear on the scene. But no one makes an effort to enter the bus, instead they wait for the SWAT team to arrive. This is to prevent more people from getting hurt. Vincent is now alone in the bus for hours with Tim's lifeless body, desecrating it more and more. He starts cutting up the body and even consumes some body parts.

Almost five hours after the crime, around 01:38, Vincent moves to the back of the bus, breaks a window and tries to escape. Thus, the police finally get the chance to catch and arrest him. Vincent taunts the investigators by throwing his victim's head at their feet. The witnesses are now taken to different police stations, while the policemen take a closer look at the bus.

The images they see there will forever be burned onto their retinas. Tim's body is spread all over the bus, but that's not all. His eyes and a piece of his heart can never be found, suggesting that the perpetrator ate them. In the perpetrator's jacket pocket, police officers find Tim's nose, lips and several other body parts.

All of Canada is deeply shocked by this gruesome act and all the news channels are reporting about it non-stop. While the news are on, Tim's mother Carol is at work. She works as a cook in a retirement home. She already has a bad feeling in her stomach at lunchtime, but she can't place it. In the evening she is at the retirement home to prepare dinner. Together with the seniors, she prays for the family of the deceased, without knowing that the man who was killed was her own son. After the prayer is said, she says: "That could have been my son.

In the evening, Tim is expected by his father, Tim McLean Senior. His son had previously lived with him and his wife, Nadine. To please his son, he gets him his favorite meal: a bucket of fried chicken. When he arrives home with the food in his luggage, however, it is not his son who is waiting for him there, but his son's friends. They ask him if he has already heard what happened? Tim's father says no and asks a counter question; he wants to know what is supposed to have happened.

Together, the friends accompany the confused father into the house and tell Tim McLean Senior to take a seat in front of the PC. Once he is seated, they show him the headlines; show him what happened to his son. From that moment on, everything is different, and his life is turned upside down from one second to the next.

Around 7:30 p.m. Tim McLean Senior calls his ex-wife and gives her the news that the boy from the bus is their common son. It is not officially confirmed at this point, but everyone knows. Carol cannot and will not believe that her son is no longer alive.

She yells at her ex-husband; tells him to stop saying things like that, to just stop. After the phone call, she feels like she's going to throw up. She tears open the front door and lets her emotions run wild, she screams; screams out the pain with all her might. All this cannot be true. A short time later, the police officially confirm that the murdered man is indeed Tim McLean.

Now we have to wait, wait for the trial of the man who took Tim McLean out of life far too early. But who is Vincent Li anyway? In 2001, the man and his wife Anna set off from China to Canada - to the city of Winnipeg. They spend a total of 5 years there. Despite his degree in computer science Vincent has difficulties to find a job in this field in his new home country, instead he only finds rather badly paid jobs.

Between October and November 2004, Vincent goes to Grant Memorial Baptist Church in Winnipeg, hoping to perhaps find a new job there. His search is successful, he starts working there as a night watchman and carries out this job for 6 months. In addition, he is baptized and converts to Christianity. From the summer of 2005, Vincent works as a forklift driver at Midland Foods on Narin Avenue, also in Winnipeg. Meanwhile, his wife works in a restaurant and regularly attends Grant Memorial Baptist Church with her husband.

But disputes between the couple become more and more frequent. Divorce follows. Vincent himself now turns his back on Winnipeg and moves to Edmonton. Another year later Vincent receives Canadian citizenship. He obtains this since he has lived and worked in Canada for at least 3 years without incident.

After the separation from Anna, he changes his jobs more often: once he delivers newspapers, another time he works as a cashier in a grocery store. Vincent was often noticed by his colleagues as being somewhat confused but was never aggressive.

On July 29, 2008, he boards a bus to Winnipeg with a few bags and his computer in his luggage. But instead of ending the trip at his planned destination, Vincent leaves the bus in Erickson and sits down on a bench where he spends the next night.

While spending time on the bench, he decides to sell his laptop for $600 (445 GBP) and makes a sign to advertise his offer. His plan takes effect, and a teenager quickly expresses interest in the computer. Right at the beginning, however, he remarks that he can't come up with the $600 asked. Vincent asks him how much money he has on him and when the boy replies with "60 dollars!" (about 45 GBP), Vincent does not hesitate for long, but sells the boy his computer for 60 dollars.

On the evening of July 30, 2008, he then boards Greyhound Bus 1170 to continue his journey, and so the paths of the perpetrator and the victim cross. All of Canada wonders which motive drove the perpetrator. Tim McLean did not know his killer and he had done nothing during the bus ride that could have provoked his seatmate in any way. Only Vincent himself can answer this question and that is exactly what he does; quite openly and honestly.

He begins to talk about the voices in his head. Voices in his head that warn him of evil people, and one of these voices he can identify exactly: it is the voice of God. He says that God instructed him to leave the bus in Erickson and wait there. He says that he is the evil son of a wicked god who has chosen him as a killer and Tim as a victim. He cannot answer the question of why he, of all people, was chosen. He only knows that God would control all people. Only God himself knows the reasons for this. It was God who gave him the order to cut up Tim's body. If he did not do that, Tim would come back to life and kill him. Vincent wants to take full responsibility for what he did. Although God told him what to do, it was his hands that killed Tim McLean. He wants the death penalty for himself because that is the only just punishment. When he learns that the death penalty does not exist in Canada, he becomes angry.

Vincent Li is diagnosed with schizophrenia. For him, the psychiatrist's finding is no surprise, as he was already diagnosed with the mental illness in 2005. However, he did not treat the illness at that time. On August 5, 2008, Vincent stands trial for the first time in Portage La Prairie, charged with second-degree murder. On March 05, 2009, the verdict is handed down in Winnipeg. Vincent is not held criminally responsible for the murder; the defense and prosecution agree on his state of mind and consider him not guilty of the crime. Judge John Scurfield says Vincent did not know he was acting morally wrong, thinking he was acting in self-defense. Instead of jail, he will now be housed at Selkirk Mental Health Center.

Carol, Tim's mother, files a lawsuit in civil court against the offender, the bus company, the Canadian police and the Canadian government. She says the perpetrator should never have entered the bus with the hunting knife. In addition, to this day she is shocked by the behavior of the police officers on the scene. She can't believe the police officers allowed Vincent Li to eat parts of her son. She says the loss is bad enough but knowing that no one even tried to stop him makes it all worse to bear.

To this day, the family is haunted by nightmares. It is impossible to describe how much Tim is missed by them. His father has a picture of his son tattooed on his chest to keep him with him at all times.

The crime also left its mark on the police officers on duty who were present on the scene that day. In 2014, one of the police officers took his own life due to Post Traumatic Stress Disorder. The people who were on the 1170 bus with Vincent and Tim are also still struggling with the aftermath from that night. Some of them are paranoid and introverted. They avoid crowds and have difficulty opening up. As soon as they close their eyes, they are haunted by nightmares; they will never be able to forget Tim's screams. When they are in crowds, they keep looking around: there could be another person who just goes berserk for no reason and maybe this time attacks them.

In 2016, Tim's family comes to an incomprehensible decision. Vincent Li is released from the psychiatric hospital, receives a new name and his criminal record remains without entries. At the beginning, he has to undergo regular checks to see if he is taking his medication every day.

According to the court, Vincent Li no longer poses any danger to the public and therefore he does not have to comply with any conditions in the meantime. Carol has no words for the court's decision. She fought to the very end to keep Vincent from being released. To no avail.

One should never go see a doctor without knowing their favorite diagnosis.

- Henry Fielding (1707-1754), British novelist, satirist, journalist and lawyer -

CHAPTER 9

Wild dreams

Joana hears his footsteps. She knows exactly when it's him and when it's someone else. Mom's footsteps and those of her siblings are quick and clumsy. They also go past her room, either to the bathroom at the end of the hall, or down the stairs where the kitchen is. But he slowly and heavily puts his feet in front of each other and stops in front of her door. Then silence follows, for a few seconds, before he quietly opens her door, enters, and gently closes it behind him. He doesn't speak a word as he comes up to her. There are exactly five steps to her bed. When Joana concentrates on counting them, she doesn't even notice the prick of the syringe her stepfather gives her. Nor does she feel his big, burly body rubbing against her 14-year-old child's body, his bulk on her tender weight, the ripping of the condom wrapper and everything he does afterward except through a tunnel.

"Trick or treat!" Candice clenches and grinds her jaw as a group of knee-high ghosts, witches and gloomily dressed monsters stand before her. It's Halloween 1992, and it's been cold and dark for days, even the first sub-zero temperatures are making themselves felt in October. But in the young, pretty mother with the otherwise friendly smile... blazes a rage so heated that it could melt the first black ice of the year without effort. But bravely, the dark blonde woman pulls the corners of her mouth up into a smile. After all, the children of Kipling, Saskatchewan, a village of 1,000, can't help their own personal horror - they're celebrating Halloween, a holiday she once loved, too, and one her own daughter will celebrate in a few years, when she's big enough. "You guys know this is a gas station, right?" she asks the group with a grin. "And the gas station has the best candy ever!" a dinosaur shrieks at her, so excited that his dinosaur crown bounces up and down. Candice grins and generously reaches into the boxes of Reese's candy bars and Skittles. She'll probably have to take that out of her paycheck later, but the kids' fun has cheered her up - and that's almost priceless after an evening like this.

After the gang of kids leaves the gas station, Candice's thoughts circle around her new boyfriend, Danny. It all started with the birth of their daughter nearly a year ago. Little Jade's real father only holds that title on paper. He made off right away when Candice told him about her pregnancy. At that time, a world collapsed for her. Single mother at the age of 22 - this was definitely not how she had imagined her life. But it didn't take her long to realize that you can't really plan anything in life. When she held little Jade in her arms for the first time, the world stopped for a moment. All thoughts of the biological child's father were forgotten; all that mattered was the perfect little bundle whose life depended on Candice. Today, the young woman's maternal happiness is not the classic one - Candice is not married, does not live in a house with a garden, and does not have a dog - but it is real. Jade is the reason she gets up early every morning, spends as much time as possible with her baby, and earns money at the gas station on evenings and nights. While she works, her parents watch over Jade.,. They have supported their daughter from the beginning and have never left her side. And then there's Danny. Candice was so happy when she met him a few months after Jade was born. He was more charming than any man she has ever met. Pregnancy changes the body. She suffered a lot from these changes at first. When she looked in the mirror, she saw sagging boobs, a flabby potbelly, and pale skin that had lost all tone. But through Danny's eyes, she felt beautiful, feminine and desirable again. Not much older than her, he lives in the next town and has the most beautiful brown eyes. He has always been affectionate with little Jade, too. For a few months, Candice was on cloud nine. But now it turns out that Danny can also be safely put in the "pigs" drawer. Apparently, words like "the only one", "forever" and "only you" have a different meaning for him than they do for her. Friends of Candice's have observed Danny making eyes at other women and wooing them several times in the past. Although Candice is hurt by this, she has always been able to dismiss his behaviour with a casual "That's men...". But now he has finally gone too far. He invited another woman to dinner. The two were seen together in a restaurant, laughing, flirting. A real date. Candice was already yelling and insulting him on the phone. Emotional control is not one of her strong points, and especially not when it comes to Danny. Everything could have been so beautiful. But apparently, she was attracting irresponsible and commitment-phobic men like a magnet. On the phone, Danny was still trying to justify himself, affirming that he would like to come by the gas station after Candice's shift to talk about everything. She locks the register, turns off the lights and pulls the grille in front of the front door. Danny's black van is already in the parking lot.

Half an hour later, tears run hot down her cheeks, leaving black trails of mascara and eyeliner. Candice's belly burns like fire. The feeling is so strong she thinks it will rip her insides apart. She can't bring herself to think clearly, standing helpless and lost in front of the gas station down the street. It's true, Danny has fallen in love with someone else. Candice should let him have "a little freedom" and everything would be all right. Her indescribable anger is joined by a feeling of disappointment, and self-doubt also comes a-knocking. Maybe it's her, probably she's not good enough, her and her flabby, sagging belly. Candice, despite the emotional chaos she's going through on this Halloween night, realizes that she can't go home in her current state. She is no longer alone but is in charge of her young daughter's life. Her thoughts turn to her friend Marie, who works as a nurse at Kipling Medical Center. Maybe she can help her, either by talking to her or with a sedative.

Carry is a sturdy woman. She is just right for the job at the front desk of Kipling Medical Center, and she has worked there for ten years. She has seen numerous emergencies and serious injuries in her career. But the young woman standing in front of her that night touches her in a very unique way. Her light brown hair is thick and voluminous, but it stands tousled from her head. Her brown, expressive eyes would radiate a strong aura under normal circumstances, but now they are red and puffy. Her skin is tanned and visibly clear when no smeared makeup is covering it. Carry realizes that Candice is a beauty. She is sorry to see her in this distraught, distressed state, and then to have to tell her that her friend Marie is not on duty today. Carry feels an urgent need to help Candice. The least she can do is offer her a checkup with the doctor who is on the night shift tonight. Seemingly, this suggestion actually calms the young woman. She says Dr. Schneeberger has already delivered her daughter, Jade.

Candice holds Dr. Schneeberger in high regard. He accompanied her during her pregnancy and eventually delivered Jade. Dr. John Schneeberger is one of those men that all heads turn to when he walks into a room, and then he can completely take over that room for himself. He is tall and of an athletic build. His dark hair is thick, something not all of his peers are blessed with. In his mid-30s, he has already achieved quite a bit. Candice knows about this as he told her about it during his physicals. He was born and raised a white male in what is now Zambia, South Africa. That sunny place has also translated to his disposition. He smiles often, revealing a row of bright white, straight teeth. After his education at the best local private colleges, he immediately found employment in Kipling. His medical career is in full swing, and while the profession is fulfilling enough for most doctors, Dr. Schneeberger is involved locally and socially. A fund he created helped open a swimming pool in Kipling. But even without actions like these, he would be popular with the residents of the small town. He enjoys chatting with everyone he meets on the street and always meets everyone in a friendly and interested manner. Of course, his good looks also play a role in the fact that especially the women of the town like to get involved in a conversation with the successful doctor. But his heart is already taken. The lucky one is called Lisa, and since last year at the latest she is considered Kipling's most envied wife, because now she is not only Dr. Schneeberger's partner, but also wears a golden wedding ring on her finger. Lisa is an attractive and also friendly woman who has already brought two children into the relationship from a previous marriage. Their two daughters together with John complete their picture-perfect family - a family that fits perfectly in a peaceful small town like Kipling. Candice is relieved when Dr. Schneeberger enters the treatment room. She knows she looks terrible. In the room, a mirror hangs on the wall above the small sink in the corner. There, she caught a glimpse of her puffy face, smeared makeup and red eyes. But Dr. Schneeberger doesn't let on. Friendly and charming as always, he asks her to tell him what happened. And Candice tells him. Again and again, her eyes fill with fresh tears, and she is ashamed of them. Her doctor doesn't interrupt her once, just nods understandingly now and then. At the end of her story, however, his expression changes. Candice recognizes concern and seriousness in his otherwise bright eyes. He listens to her with a stethoscope and measures her blood pressure. It is slightly elevated, and her pulse is also too fast. Otherwise, she is physically unharmed, fortunately, but as a precaution he gives her an injection. A sedative, so that her heartbeat would normalize, and she could calm down. Candice thinks of Jade and wants to agree with her doctor. But he apparently does not understand his suggestion as such, but as a decision. He has already gotten up and disappeared from the room. After a few minutes, he returns, closes the door and applies the syringe to her upper arm. Candice still wants to ask what exactly he is injecting her, but her mouth can no longer form words. She feels dizzy and as if she were standing in a tunnel.

The next morning, Candice wakes up in a hospital bed. Completely disoriented, she looks from left to right, raises and lowers her head, but these movements trigger violent dizziness in her. "Where am I?" she mumbles over and over, but no one hears her. Only after long minutes do the fragments in her head come together to form a complete picture. The snow-white walls, the equally bright bedding with its sterile smell, and the linoleum floor - she's still in the hospital. Candice feels weak, she also has unexplained pain in her abdomen. She knows she broke up with Danny and was examined at Kipling Medical Center by Dr. Schneeberger. But didn't he really just want to inject her with a sedative so she could relax and go home safely? Why isn't she in her own bed, with her daughter in the crib right next to her? "Pull yourself together," she inwardly talks to herself for courage. Despite dizziness and weakness, she mobilizes her strength and swings her legs out of bed. Just as she is about to get up and look for a nurse, her room door opens. Dr. Schneeberger wishes her a good morning and gives her his broad smile. But for Candice it is not a good morning, not at all. Instinctively, she senses that something terrible has happened to her. "What did you inject me with yesterday?" she asks her doctor directly. The latter answers her with a laugh. When Candice doesn't join in, he asks back, "Why do you ask? Did it give you wild dreams?"

The fresh air does her good. Candice feels her energy reserves being replenished with each breath. Once she got out of bed, she quickly felt better and strong enough to leave the hospital. She remembers. She doesn't remember exactly what happened, but she is sure that something bad was done to her last night. When she arrives home, she is greeted by her parents, her dear mother and her kind-hearted father, who were already worried sick - where had she gone last night? Candice confides in them both. "Dr. Schneeberger. He abused me."

Candice tells her parents the whole story. About the kids trick-or-treating at the gas station, about her breakup with Danny and the stay at Kipling Medical Center. That Dr. Schneeberger gave her a shot that didn't contain a sedative, but something else. A substance that knocked her out. But the memories came back, slowly at first, and then full force. Candice stood beside herself after the injection, becoming an observer of the cruel spectacle in which her motionless body itself played the leading role. Her doctor rubbed his body against hers, then pulled out a condom and penetrated her. Dr. Schneeberger raped her. The man she trusted to deliver her daughter abused her trust, her body and her soul. As she narrates, her parents listen in silence, but their faces say it all. Of course, they believe their daughter and are determined to stand by her side during this difficult time, again, just as they did during her pregnancy. And yet, Dr. Schneeberger, of all people? The kind, friendly doctor and family man who is so exemplary in his commitment to the city and enjoys boundless popularity everywhere?

Candice sits in the back seat of her father's car. He and her mother are driving her to Regina, the next town over. She wants to get checked at the hospital there. She can't return to the Kipling Medical Center for that. But she needs the proof in black and white. Candice trusts herself, and she trusts her parents. She appreciates that they have stood by her side as always and said nothing.

But she has seen it in their faces, that tiny hint of doubt. And she can't blame them. Dr. Schneeberger is untouchable in Kipling. The next five hours cost Candice all her strength once again. She has to undress completely. Hair and blood samples are taken, along with swabs from all her orifices. But at the end of the procedure, she has the proof. There is sperm in her vagina and on her panties. The last time she slept with Danny was several weeks ago.

The investigators know Dr. John Schneeberger. A nice man, well-liked everywhere. He has settled into their community very well and has a harmonious marriage. His children do well in school and are involved in the town's sports clubs. They are embarrassed to appoint the doctor to the presidency. But of course, they have to follow up on the young woman's complaint. Now Dr. Schneeberger is sitting across from them, wearing jeans and a cashmere sweater. If he feels offended or is annoyed by the summons, he doesn't let on. Smiling amiably, he looks at her over the rim of his glasses, legs crossed, hands open on the table. Candice's accusations against him are, of course, completely groundless. The young mother, he says, showed up at his house in the middle of the night in a worrisome state. Crying and in a rage over which she herself had no control. Therefore, he gave her a shot of Dormicum, a follow-up drug to Valium. It has a sedative effect but is often accompanied by hallucinations. The sexual assault was therefore pure imagination, a side effect of the injection. Besides, there were nurses on duty everywhere - in the corridor, at the reception, in the rooms. If Candice's accusations were true, they would have heard about it. Of course, he immediately agrees to a blood test anyway, he would take care of it directly at the hospital. After all, he doesn't want to jeopardize his reputation. And indeed: the DNA of the sperm in Candice's panties and vagina does not match that of Dr. Schneeberger's blood.

In a small town like Kipling, news spreads like wildfire. The residents are outraged by the accusations against their esteemed Dr. Schneeberger. The entire village, including the police officers, are behind him. Even his wife Lisa does not leave his side. She explains Candice's behavior with jealousy. Her husband is extremely attractive and successful. This young woman is certainly not the first unhappy lover, but definitely the first to resort to such unscrupulous means to destroy the Schneeberger family.

Candice stands in front of the crib and looks at her sleeping daughter. Seeing Jade in such a peaceful state fills her with peace herself. Dr. Schneeberger's DNA does not match that of the sperm. The whole village thinks she is a lovesick, desperate lunatic who has it in for the popular doctor. A doubt briefly germinates in her mind. Was she perhaps mistaken after all? In a matter of seconds, this thought vanishes again. She knows exactly that she hasn't had sexual intercourse with Danny for weeks. It must have been Dr. Schneeberger. He must have mixed up his blood sample with another one. Maybe even the entire hospital staff is in cahoots.

Candice struggles, but resistance is strong. The popular gynecologist enjoys the full backing of Kipling, his wife and the police. For them, the matter was already concluded following the blood test. The world around her continues to turn, her daughter is one year older. She doesn't give up, and in August 1993 the police finally agree to ask Dr. Schneeberger for a second blood test. That's because the officers have to admit that they weren't present the first time. It was not them who took the doctor's blood, but he himself, and it was analyzed directly at Kipling Medical Center. This time the blood is taken from the doctor in the presence of the investigators, right in front of them. An hour later, the result is available. They apologize to Dr. Schneeberger for the inconvenience, bid him a good day and put the case to rest.

Candice is stunned. There is no thought of giving up, because she is sure of herself. She realizes that there are rocks in her path - big, heavy boulders that she can't roll out of the way on her own to get to her destination. Therefore, she seeks help from someone with more resources than her own hands and hires a private investigator. Larry O'Brien believes every word the young woman says. During his long career as a private investigator, he has met some superficially perfect family men with flawless records and prestige who have more than one body hiding in their basement. He is also no stranger to police work. From their side, they have done everything in their power to investigate the allegations of the alleged victim. But the evidence is clear, Dr. Schneeberger is innocent. Larry knows that just because a blood sample doesn't match another DNA doesn't mean anything. He watches the doctor for a few days but sees nothing unusual. While working at the hospital one afternoon, Larry breaks into his car in the Kipling Medical Center parking lot unnoticed - jackpot. He finds a lip balm and a comb with hair caught in it.

At her own expense and with Larry's help, Candice has the lip balm and hair tested at the lab. The hairs turn out to be useless because they contain no roots. But the DNA of the skin flakes found on the lip balm match the DNA of the sperm.

Candice feels like she's running a marathon, advancing in first place only to fall just before the finish line. The evidence, due to Larry breaking into Dr. Schneeberger's car, is illegitimate. It also raises the question of whether the doctor actually uses lip balm regularly. But Candice continues not to give up. She files suit in civil court to revoke Dr. Schneeberger's license. So, on November 20, 1996, the doctor sits in police headquarters again, this time with a running camera. When the nurse wants to take blood from his finger, Dr. Schneeberger insists with a friendly smile that he should take his arm instead - he would quickly get hematomas on his hands, and as a doctor he needs them. After Dr. Schneeberger has left the room, the nurse hesitantly looks at the blood sample, holds it against the light, swings it back and forth. When asked by the police officers, she explains, "The blood looks kind of strange, like it's not fresh."

In fact, the blood cannot be evaluated. The case is shelved again.

Lisa Schneeberger almost forgot about Candice. For half a year, peace and quiet have finally reigned in her family. But illusions are deceptive. April 25, 1997, not only puts her world back into turmoil and trouble, but this time it turns to rubble. She doesn't suspect it yet as she happily stands in the kitchen preparing salad dressing for dinner. John is working tonight, but her children are all home. She looks forward to spending time together. "Would you like to help me, sweetheart?" she gleefully asks as her 15-year-old daughter, Joana, enters the kitchen. At first, she doesn't notice her depressed face. Only when a tear runs down Joana's cheek does Lisa put down the salad servers and take her daughter in her arms. Shortly after, her fragile little girl whimpers, "Mama, he did it to me, too."

During Joana's narration, Lisa is in a state of limbo. She knows she is sitting on her bed in her daughter's room, her child tightly in her arms. Yet she feels so helpless, wondering how it could have come to this. Why did she, as a mother, not notice all this time. But she immediately believes her daughter's every word, what mother would doubt that? Joana shows her a silver square bag. A condom wrapper. Several times a week for nearly two years now, John has been coming into his stepdaughter's room at night and administering shots to make her compliant. Maybe her body got used to the drug, because at one point Joana could remember what happened the next morning. And a few weeks later she got to see it all, as if through a tunnel, as a bystander. Only she was not a spectator, but the victim of numerous rapes.

Crying and broken inside, Lisa scrapes together her strength. For the sake of her children, she talks herself into courage. She tears John's clothes out of the closet in the bedroom and stuffs everything in batches into suitcases and travel bags. But one of the suitcases seems heavier to her than the others, and it is already packed. Inside, Lisa finds a number of syringes, liquid substances in glass containers and countless condoms. The sight of these items causes vivid images in her mind, of her husband, in bed with their 15-year-old daughter. Disgusted, hateful and full of self-reproach, she drops everything and calls the police. After taking Joana's statement and recovering the medical kit, they arrest Dr. John Schneeberger while he is still working the night shift at Kipling Medical Center. Under the suspicious and incredulous looks of the hospital staff, they lead the doctor away.

Once at the presidential office, there is no sign of the friendly Dr. Schneeberger. A wrinkle of anger forms between his otherwise bright, open eyes. He sits opposite the officers with his lips pressed tightly together and his arms folded, not saying a word. He does not want to comment further on the accusations. The police officers realize that they have caught him this time. Now they take blood from the doctor's fingers and use hair samples. A few hours later, the results are in, and the cops contact Candice by return mail. She didn't lie, and she didn't imagine anything. Dr. Schneeberger's DNA clearly matches the DNA of the semen found in her panties and vagina at the time.

Until his trial began in November 1999, the accused medical doctor remained silent. That' s how long the investigators, Candice and Lisa have to wait for an answer to the all-important question: How can it be that the first three blood samples did not already convict him?

Dr. Schneeberger presents his version of the story in court. It is so unbelievable that the jury initially does not believe him. He had implanted a capsule with the blood of another patient into his arm in order to falsify the samples. The doctor's insanity is true. On the video recordings of the third blood sample, an elevation in his arm can be seen quite clearly, and the nurse's comment that the blood looks strange and not fresh also supports the theory. After the trial day, which brought the truth to light, the capsule is promptly removed from the defendant. The next day, it lies on the table as evidence before the judge, who questions Dr. Schneeberger as to why. How does a smart, well-liked, dedicated family man and doctor come to implant himself with a capsule containing the blood of a stranger? Dr. Schneeberger pleads self-protection. Candice is one of his numerous admirers, but she has gone too far. She broke into his home, stole a used condom from the trash and blackmailed him with it. She had wanted to claim that he used the condom with her to destroy his family. No one in the audience or on the bench believes him. He is sentenced to six years in prison. It has taken seven years for Candice to fight for the truth.

Lisa feels relief after the verdict is announced. However, six years is nothing compared to a human life. After all, the trauma her still-husband did to her Joana and Candice will likely follow the two women for the rest of their lives. The day after John's incarceration, she files for divorce and, through her lawyer, forbids him to have any contact with the two daughters they share.

John does not accept the ban on contact. He has Lisa informed through his attorney that he has a right to see his children despite what he has done. For rehabilitation purposes, Canadian law supports contact between children and their delinquent parents. Lisa endures the lecture from John's lawyer over the phone. He had also sent her a letter for her records summarizing the legal basis and the facts of the case. Lisa hangs up, and it is clear to her: never will she endanger any more of her children by letting them near the sex offender who was once the love of her life.

After the first $2,000 fine Lisa receives for the unlawful no-contact order, she begins her fight. She files a lawsuit against the sentence for ten long weeks. But she loses. The law is the law, and her case is no exception. From now on, she must allow her ex-husband to visit their two common girls every last Sunday of the month.

In May 2001, Lisa and the two children they share are standing outside the prison where her ex-husband is serving time. The six- and seven-year-old girls each cling to one of their mother's hands. Lisa senses that they are afraid. A prison is no place for children. After the strong media coverage of the case, which reached beyond the country's borders, hundreds of people gathered in front of the entrance to make a statement. They symbolically block the gates. Among the peaceful demonstrators, however, are no residents of Kipling - they continue to stand loyally by their beloved doctor. Lisa pauses in awe for a few seconds. She is moved by so much solidarity. At that moment, with an uncomfortable tug in her stomach, she thinks of Candice, the young woman she has denied this very help over the years. She is terribly sorry. She could not protect Joana, did not believe Candice, and even now she cannot spare her two youngest daughters the visits to her ex-husband. Helplessly, she advances with slow steps towards the entrance. But in the entrance hall, the little girls already start crying at her hand. They cling tightly to her legs and sob that they want to go home. The sight of her two youngest girls breaks Lisa's heart. How is she supposed to explain to them that there are laws here in Canada that even as a mother she can't go against? But before she has to give an answer that will never be enough, a social worker steps in. She cannot justify forcing the girls to visit under these circumstances. The family is allowed to go home.

A few days after the incident, Lisa discovers an envelope from jail in her mailbox. It is a letter from John, who informs her that he will refrain from further visits from his two daughters.

In 2003, after four years in prison, John is released on parole. His medical license is irretrievably revoked. He settles in Regina, Kipling's neighboring village, and works for a construction company. But the tenuous beginnings of his new life come to an abrupt end after a few months of freedom. Authorities discover that he lied when he applied for Canadian citizenship in 1993. When asked if he had been charged with a crime or convicted of an offense, he put his check mark at "no." Candice reported him for sexual abuse as early as November 1992. This misinformation is enough to send Dr. Schneeberger back to South Africa.

In July 2004, John's plane lands in Zambia. He moves in with his mother and works in a catering company for a few years. Today, he trains new sommeliers at the Durban Wine Academy. His ex-wife Lisa spends a lot of time with their now grown-up children. The two daughters do not seek contact with their father.

Candice is happily married and works as an assistant in an addiction counseling center. She loves her job. For years she felt herself a lost soul, misunderstood and alone. But today her experiences help her patients and give them courage: Never give up, justice will prevail in the end.

»Bullying is a mental crime in instalments.«

*- Franz Schmidberger (*1942), German journalist -*

CHAPTER 10

Under the bridge

(By Lisa Bielec / Mordgeflüster der Podcast)

It is already quite cold on this morning of November 14, 1997.... But her excitement alone makes Reena warm. Reena is not one of those teenagers who have many friends. Quite the opposite, in fact, she never makes friends. Meeting new people is insanely difficult for her. That's why it's not surprising how excited she is to be part of a unit. It's not just any clique, it's that kind of group that everyone wants to be friends with. She's nailed it. Friday evenings are the highlight of the week for her. That' s where the teens get together pretty much every week. Tonight, it's that time again.

The clique is made up of a whole bunch of teens who meet regularly either at the local school or at Craigflower Bridge. This gang is one of those that parents warn their children about, that you definitely don't want to have trouble with and would prefer to change the side of the street.

Reena has also changed since she became a part of them. She has become rebellious; starts using alcohol and drugs. This behavior is difficult to bear for her conservative parents. Her father is an immigrant from India, and her mother is Indo-Canadian. The family converts from Hinduism to Jehovah's Witnesses after arriving in Canada.

Jehovah's Witnesses live by strict rules. For example, members are not allowed to have sex before marriage, they completely reject blood transfusion treatment, and they do not celebrate birthdays or other Christian holidays. They also lead a rather conservative life-anything but what a teenager would have in mind.

Reena would like to defy this way of life. She wants to live like all her peers do. To achieve this, Reena makes a momentous decision in 1996. In order to escape her family and live a looser life, Reena reports her father for sexual abuse. She is taken into the custody of the state and hopes to be placed in a foster home. However, she quickly realizes what she has done to her family and drops the charges. The girl returns home.

Reena, however, wants to finally escape loneliness and experience acceptance after years of being a victim of bullying. She had constantly experienced rejection because of her weight or insecurity from her peers. Reena hopes to get a lot out of these new friendships.

But there have already been not-so-good times, too. Just recently, she had had severe problems. She had been accused of stealing Nicole Cook's phone book and then making calls to Nicole's friends and spreading rumors. She was also alleged to have made a pass at a classmate's boyfriend. The girls accusing her of this are also part of the group. But apparently the problem has since been resolved. Or has it?

Today, she doesn't want to think about what happened. Today she wants to keep the feelings of happiness that she has already had after getting up. Reena counts the hours until she can finally set off. That's how long she has been waiting to finally make friends. She dresses up in something warm, because it is very cold that day.

In the late afternoon, Reena sets off for Shoreline School in View Royal, where the teenagers always meet in the field behind the school building.

Reena's home is in Saanich, in the province of British Columbia. The Canadian province is located right on the coast of the Pacific Ocean and stands out for its natural beauty. There are breath-taking lakes that could not be bluer or more beautiful. British Columbia offers natural sceneries that look like they were painted. Saanich is a medium-sized city. You can find everything you need here, but it is not that village-like that everybody knows everybody. Saanich is known for its small quiet harbor.

As Reena steps out the door, she takes a deep breath of the cold, wintry air. As she exhales, her breath becomes visible. Catching her breath does her good. It was a good idea to put on the jacket, Reena thinks to herself as she starts walking.

She passes fashion stores and supermarkets. From a distance, she can see the harbor. She watches some people on her way; sees couples strolling through the streets, other passers-by standing in front of the shop windows.

The hours had passed so slowly, as always when you are looking forward to something special. A feeling of happiness makes itself broad, the closer she comes to the meeting place.

Arriving at the field, there' hardly enough time to say 'hello' to everyone, as the police arrive quite quickly. This happens more and more often on Fridays.

For the teenagers, however, this is not a problem, they just move on to the Craigflower Bridge, which is not too far away.

Under that bridge, you're a bit more sheltered from the wind anyway. For Reena, the only thing that matters is that she can be part of it. Whether it's in a field or under a bridge. Immediately after arrival, alcohol is drunk and drugs are consumed. Reena feels good, she enjoys being with the other teenagers. Enjoys finally not having to spend her Friday nights on her own. At last, she can be like any other teenager. This feeling of freedom inspires her. What might it be like in the summer when the temperatures are slightly higher? She realizes that she is in for a good time.

After arriving at the place under the bridge, chaos suddenly erupts amongst them. Nicole, the girl Reena is supposed to have spread the rumors about, immediately goes after her. She stubs a cigarette butt out on Reena's forehead. A crowd quickly forms around her. Not only Nicole, but also six other girls and a boy attack her.

Reena did not expect this. She goes down, now lying in the mud at the feet of her attackers.

She is beaten and kicked over and over again. Even against her head several times. She is bleeding. She apologizes for what she is supposed to have done. Many teenagers stand around the group and watch as Reena is tortured by her tormentors. No one offers help, even though she obviously needs it. The scene resembles a movie, a pretty bad movie.

Eventually, the teens let go of her after a girl present is able to get the group to stop beating her. Reena is able to stagger and save herself onto the bridge. What on earth had just happened? She had been looking forward to the evening so much, and now this. She hadn't expected such a turn of events.

Reena's entire body aches. She feels like she can feel every inch of it. Her muscles ache, her skin burns, and she is bleeding. She just wants to go home.

Oh God, home. How is she going to explain what happened to her parents? They'll probably never let her out again. Reena feels very uneasy. Reena can't understand how the mood could change so quickly and how the others in the group could be so brutal.

Reena is still in thought and stumbling along when she is attacked again. Two of the attackers have followed her. 15-year-old Kelly Ellard and 16-year-old Warren Glowatski go after her again. They drag her to the opposite side of the street. There they force the girl to take off her clothes. Then Warren and Kelly start hitting Reena again several times.

Even the fact that Reena is moaning in pain and keeps asking them to let go of her doesn't stop them. When is it all going to stop? Over and over again she asks the two teenagers to leave her alone.

Then her head is smashed hard against a tree. Reena falls unconscious.

The bridge becomes very quiet. So quiet that it is almost eerie. No more sounds of pain. No pleading. Just the sound of rushing water and the distant sounds of the other teens echoing through the darkness.

A plan must be made. They can't leave the motionless girl lying here. What happened must be covered up.

To get rid of Reena, Warren and Kelly throw her into the Gorge Waterway, whose November temperatures are anything but mild. In doing so, the two set the seal on Reena's death sentence. As if nothing else had happened, they return to the rest of the group still under the bridge. They agree that no one saw anything, and everyone should keep their mouths shut.

In for a penny, in for a pound. They continue with the evening.

Reena does not return home that evening. Her parents are very worried after only a short time. Although their daughter is currently rebellious and not very reliable, this is not like her. They turn to the police, who then immediately begin their search.

Rumors of a murder spread rapidly, however, and it is the number one topic of conversation on Monday at Shoreline Middle School. Reena was a student at nearby Colquitz Middle School. Several uninvolved students, as well as teachers, learn of the rumor, but no one reports it to the police.

In the meantime, police are combing through woods, they are also interviewing teenagers who were at the said site that evening. Gorge Waterway is also searched again by the police officers.

Eight days after the crime, on November 22, 1997, police divers find Reena's half-naked body and recover it from the lake.

Immediately, her body is brought to the forensics department and examined in detail. It quickly becomes clear that the young girl has been the victim of a violent crime. Countless injuries adorn her body.

One sees several burns caused by cigarette butts. In addition, the forensic pathologist notes that an attempt must have been made to set Reena's hair on fire. There are charred areas all over her head. The medical examiner also discovers bruises on the teenager's head and abdomen.

After his autopsy, the medical examiner concludes that Reena has drowned. However, he notes that Reena's head injuries had been so severe that she would have died from them anyway.

Possible perpetrators can be quickly located based on witness testimony, and so in February 1998, six of the girls and Warren are charged. They have to answer for their actions in court.

Since this case involves teenagers, their identities are to be deliberately protected. The Juvenile Justice Act stipulates this. The girls should remain capable of rehabilitation because they were very young at the time of the crime. From then on, the group of girls is called the 'Shoreline Six'. Only their initials are made public.

Three of the perpetrators plead guilty to assault. Kelly and Warren, given the seriousness of the crime, are tried in adult court.

In addition to Warren and Kelly, Nicole Cook, Missy Grace Pleich, Nicole Patterson, Courtney Keith and Gail Ooms are charged. One girl in the group attempts suicide. She is in no condition to be transferred to a jail.

In court, the circumstances of the accused teens are elaborated. Each of the teens couldn't be more different.

Warren has had a difficult upbringing. His mother is an alcoholic and absent most of the time. At the time of the crime, he was living with a friend. His father meets a woman in Los Angeles and eventually moves there. Warren wants to stay in Saanich and from then on lives in a trailer. He lives off the money his father sends him. Warren Glowatski is sentenced to life in prison. His appeal is rejected in 2001.

Warren takes responsibility for his crime while in prison. He participates in restorative justice programs and supports programs designed to reunite offenders and victims of crimes against Indigenous people. While in custody, he himself learns that he is Metis. This means that he is part of the Indigenous community. At one of these meetings, Warren then meets Reena's parents. He regrets the crime and apologizes to the Virks. Reena's parents are able to forgive him and by the end of the meeting, both sides are crying and even hugging.

In 2010, the Virks support Warren's parole application. He can be fully rehabilitated. The former inmate is proof that people can change.

Kelly, on the other hand, comes from a good background, she has a stable family environment that supports her even during the trial. However, it is revealed that the 15-year-old shows sociopathic traits. A jury finds her guilty of second-degree murder in 2000. However, the conviction is overturned by the Supreme Court of Canada on technical grounds. A second trial then occurs in 2004, at which Kelly insists on her innocence. She repeatedly affirms that she is not a monster. This leads to the jury being deadlocked and another mistrial. Then, at a third trial in 2005, a conviction is reached. This conviction is upheld on appeal to the Supreme Court, making it legally valid. Kelly Ellard is sentenced to life in prison.

For the first few years, Kelly maintains her plea of innocence. In prison, she continues to use drugs and repeatedly breaks the rules. After her boyfriend visits her in prison, Kelly Ellard becomes pregnant. She changes her name to Kerry Sim and gives birth to the baby in 2016. In 2020, she then becomes pregnant a second time, by the same partner. By now, she is in her late thirties. As part of a reintegration process, she receives parole from then on.

Nicole Cook, the girl Reena is said to have spread the rumors about, is not directly involved in the murder, yet she is the reason why the whole situation had escalated in the first place. Nicole and Missy Grace Pleich return to the crime scene after the murder to pick up Reena's clothes. Following this, the two force a younger roommate named Stephanie to hide the clothes in her closet. They also coerce the girl into making calls to Reena's parents.

After years of grieving, the Virks decide to forgive many of the perpetrators. They want to move forward and need the forgiveness to continue with their own healing process.

They also launch an anti-bullying campaign to raise public awareness to address bullying and teen violence. Thanks to them, the British Columbia government establishes several anti-bullying programs in schools. They also get bullying to become a topic of conversation and host meetings attended by thousands of kids, teachers and law enforcement professionals. The Virks are honored in 2009 for their contributions to crime prevention and community safety.

Suman Virk dies on June 16, 2018, at the age of 58 due to a choking attack while eating at a cafe in Victoria.

Even today, the case surrounding Reena Virk represents a change in the system. Bullying is becoming a big issue, especially in the community of Saanish, which had the population in shock. Meanwhile, there are several projects around the case. Plays have already been staged, books written, and reports produced about Reena's murder. Because one thing is clear: Reena Virk must never be forgotten, and everyone should be aware that bullying destroys human lives.

The path is smooth that leadeth on to danger.

- William Shakespeare (1564-1616)
English playwright, poet and actor -

CHAPTER 11

Survived

(by Chenoa and Saskia / Überdosis Crime)

The front door breaks open. There' s a loud bang. The owner of the farmhouse sees the silhouette of a man with a rifle standing in the doorway. He does not know what is happening. Just a moment ago, he and his wife were sitting on the edge of the bed, rocking the baby and getting ready for the new day. The clock shows 6:00 a.m. If some specialists and doctors had not been too optimistic about their patient's recovery, something terrible might have been prevented.

The birth of Victor makes the family's happiness seem perfect. He is the fifth child of Robert and Stella Hoffman. Later, there were to be seven children in total. But no matter how many siblings little Victor would have had, he would certainly have stood out from the crowd.

The Hoffmans are really just an average farming family, running a mixed farm on their own piece of land 70km from Saskatoon in Canada. Growing crops and raising livestock is the Hoffman family's bread and butter.

Soon, however, Stella and Robert's thoughts would turn not to their farm, but solely to their son.

As Victor Hoffman grows up, he seems like all the other kids his age. He is healthy, shy, and very good at keeping to himself.

When Victor is 6 years old, he starts school and quickly finds a friend. He should not have another one.

Around this time, he will later state, the little boy sees "the devil" for the first time. The figure is completely black, about 6 foot tall and has a long tail. Victor also begins to hear knocking noises, at night, after the sun has set. It seems like the knocking is getting faster and louder. To him, it feels as if he is witnessing a battle between God and the devil himself.

At the age of 10, Victor feels the desire to kill every day. Whenever he meets a new person, he has the thought and even the need to harm them.

All that takes place in his head when he is all alone, the little boy keeps to himself. Not even his parents know about his thoughts and fantasies.

It is difficult for parents to look into their child's mind when the child does not want to reveal what is going on in his thoughts. And so, Victor begins to vent his impulses on animals for the time being. At first it is cats, which he catches and tortures in every conceivable way. Later it's dogs, squirrels and just about any other animal Victor can get his hands on. He has killed several hundred squirrels.

The animals are not enough for Victor. He attacks a little boy and forces him not to tell his parents.

To his own parents, however, Victor is a great help on the farm. He has the ability to solve problems like none of his other siblings can.

Unnoticed by his parents, however, remains the fact that Victor's psyche is becoming increasingly ill.

One day, as he is eating breakfast, he hears a voice speaking to him. The devil, he calls him. "Victor, Victor!" As he leaves the house, he sees a naked creature, almost 6 feet tall, standing in front of him. " Kind of resembles a pig," he thinks to himself.

It was the devil, he says, who told him he could make him rich if he would only comply.

Victor goes on to describe that the devil demands that he kneel before him. Victor does so, but only with one knee. He thinks that this way he will get at least half of what the devil promises him.

It was foreseeable that Victor would not become rich. But he himself is firmly convinced that it is because he did not do what the devil asked him to do. That is only one of a total of 20 encounters Victor believes he has had with the devil.

Later he sees angels, mostly women, he recalls. But they speak to him just as the devil did.

When Victor fails 9th grade and has to repeat it, the school principal sets up a meeting with his parents, telling them that up to that point there had never been any problems with Victor.

The trouble he doesn't cause at school he saves for his free time. Even as a boy, he is obsessed with guns. When he is 15, he breaks into a store and steals firearms. Shortly after, he hears the knocking more clearly and loudly. Like Morse code from a supernatural dimension.

When he robs the exact same store again a year later, at the age of 17, he gets caught, ends up behind bars for 24 hours, and gets a 2-year suspended sentence on top of that. In his 20s, things get even worse.

He regularly faints and throws tantrums.

Now, he sees the devil even more often. He wants to persuade him to sell him his soul. If he did not comply, he would have to go through the process of dying millions of times.

At one point, Hoffman says, God offered him to kill the devil. If he did this, he would be taken to heaven.

Victor attempts to kill the devil several times, whether with a knife or a firearm.

By this time, Victor has completely lost control of his life and his emotional world.

When Victor is 21 years old, his family also starts to notice that something is wrong with their son's psyche.

One moment Victor is calm and thoughtful, the next aggressive and in a rage, then he laughs out loud and shortly after becomes very calm again.

It is May 27, 1967, and an ordinary Saturday on the Hoffman farm, at least that is how it seems for now. Stella Hoffman is quiet and listening. "Are those gunshots?" she wonders. When she goes to check, she sees her son Victor standing in one of the fields, firing wildly with a gun. She runs toward him, screaming for him to put the gun down. He shot the devil, Victor tells her.

Stella manages to maneuver the gun out of his hands and take it into her custody.

When Victor leaves the family's property shortly after and drives away in the car, his parents gather all sorts of weapons in the house and hide them.

But Victor, who returns home a few hours later, doesn't like this at all. He vehemently insists that no one would get hurt if they gave them back to him.

Stella and her husband order the pastor in charge to stop by their house and talk to Victor about his thoughts and feelings.

Stella tries to eavesdrop on what her son would tell the pastor but can't quite make it out. As the pastor is about to finish talking to Victor and leave, she hears her son say to him, "I'd like to kill Mother."

Now, at last, his family understands the full extent of his illness. They immediately arrange for a place in therapy at a psychiatric hospital.

In North Battleford, Victor is classified as schizoid, which means that he exhibits limited emotional expression in interpersonal relationships, often resulting in indifference.

The extent to which Victor's illness has already reached requires inpatient care in a closed psychiatric ward. At the time of his admission, Victor is initially only concerned with his psychological impairments, but his abdominal cramps and burns are secondary symptoms. These physical strains, like the burns, are most likely from the aggressive chemicals used on the farm. During the examinations, Victor is surprisingly cooperative, but exhibits increasingly withdrawn, apathetic, and indifferent behaviors as treatment progresses.

Victor only gives brief answers to questions. He tells the specialists about his interactions with the devil and the creature with the pig's head. He also states that he does not get along with his siblings very well. They would have laughed when he told them about his encounters with the devil.

He was just wondering if he was a boy or a girl, he said, since "the devil" switched his brain with a girl's named Denise. It would feel like Denise was stealing his body.

The psychiatrist classifies his experiences as hallucinations. Victor denies this, because the encounters would have been so realistic and real that they would have to be real.

The doctor also notices that Victor's daily life in the clinic is marked by sex. He masturbates on a daily basis. Although he is weak, he is unable to sleep a wink at night.

The expert diagnoses chronic schizophrenia, which manifests itself in uncontrolled symptoms and a social handicap. The classic therapy plan of the 1960s consists of antipsychotics, talk therapy and a sequence of 12 electroshock sessions. After the second application, he reportedly began to show noticeable changes. He is less withdrawn and more present, he says. The delusions, however, do not stop. After the fifth session, things probably get better again, but he is now convinced he has superpowers. After the ninth electroshock therapy, nothing has changed psychologically.

Victor's father Robert is of the opinion that Victor is psychologically back to the standard as before. By "before" is possibly meant the time when young Victor was already impaired, but his parents had not yet figured it out.

Finally, after the twelfth and last electroshock therapy, Victor denies the stories about the devil and the angels, but he would still see the devil now and then. Victor notes that if he were released again, he would try to fight the devil once more.

A few days later, his mood changes again. Now he says that his encounters were not real, although he always vehemently insisted that they were not hallucinations. Although he keeps insisting that he is free of the devil and hallucinations, Victor still often thinks about killing. However, not the devil, the creature or the angels, but his parents, siblings and friends.

Later he tells the psychiatrists that neither his friends nor his family had angered him, and he had no reason to do so at all, but he wanted to do it anyway. He is now an inpatient in the psychiatric hospital for a month when the psychiatrist phones his father and predicts that Victor's mental health could return to normal in as little as a year.

On this day, however, Victor is allowed to return home for the time being. His schizophrenia is probably "not that bad anymore." So, the psychiatrist arms Victor's father with all kinds of antipsychotics and releases the young man from the hospital in North Battleford on July 26, 1967.

The first time back home, Victor sleeps an atypical amount of time. His parents, however, consider this a good sign, as he would get enough rest and could better manage his mental illness.

But Victor is not well at all. A storm is slowly but surely bubbling up inside him. He claims to have visions where he can see what would happen far in advance. In his dreams when he sleeps, or even in his daydreams, he now thinks about killing people more often.

Two weeks after moving back home, on August 08, 1967, Victor secretly and of his own volition stops taking his hospital-prescribed medication.

The first two days, he says, he feels very well. On the third day, however, he already begins to fall back into his old behavior patterns. He knows it's not a long way until he ends up back in a closed psychiatric ward or even in jail. He says he would rather die than go back to the psychiatric hospital again. Mainly because of the electroshock therapy. He didn't really notice the first sessions because of his mental state, but after he got better and better and was more stable, the procedures were unbearable for him.

Every day after the electroshock therapy, Victor fantasized about killing.

On August 12, 1967, the thought occurs to Victor that doing something to someone would prove his abilities to the devil.

Now it is two days later, August 14, 1967, and Victor once again can't sleep, is restless and just tosses and turns in bed. He gets up and makes his way to the garage, where he spots a dog. His first thought is to kill the dog, but he doesn't.

He stays there for over an hour until he feels a sharp pain in the right side of his brain. It feels like his body is being cut straight down the middle. This pain triggers a strong impulse. For the 21-year-old it is certain - today someone will die by his hand.

Victor fills up his car, loads his rifle and drives away. The bright taillights of the car disappear in the darkness of the night.

Forty kilometers northwest of his home village is the community of Shell Lake. It's a very small town with just over 250 homes, a hotel, a small café and a pub. A narrow, unpaved and rather dirty road runs through the village.

The Peterson family, however, simply calls this place "home." The 47-year-old father of the family, James Peterson, and his 42-year-old wife, Evelyn Peterson, are very devout people who always attend church on Sundays. They live with their nine children, who range in age from 9 to 18, in a farmhouse that has five rooms. The oldest daughter, Cathy, no longer lives at home with her parents. She recently married and now lives with her husband in British Columbia. The Petersons own about 195 acres of land and father James works hard to provide for the family.

On the morning of August 15, 1967, the family is up early and getting ready for the day as Victor drives down the road with his rifle in the passenger seat. With each house Victor Hoffman drives past, his desire to kill someone increases.

The young man sees a house on the side of the road, which he believes to have seen before in one of his visions. He is sure that this is a sign. Thus, Victor drives down the driveway of the farm.

It is 6:00 in the morning. Inside the house, James and Evelyn are sitting on the edge of their bed getting ready for the new day when they hear a car door slam outside their house.

Surprised by the early visitor, James calls out, "Who's there?" but all he gets in response is the loud banging of the front door. Family man James rushes down the stairs to see what's going on down there.

Standing in the doorway is 21-year-old Victor Hoffman, who has just gained entry to the house without further trouble; in his hand is his .22 caliber rifle. Wanting to protect his family from the danger that is about to enter his house, James Peterson runs towards Victor. Four shots. All of them hit James in the stomach. As he goes down to the ground lying motionless, Victor climbs over him. Victor can hear screams coming from every room in the house.

In the living room lies 11-year-old Dorothy. As Victor approaches her, she closes her eyes. The little girl is terrified. He aims at her face and pulls the trigger.

In one of the rooms are six of the Peterson children. Mary, Pearl, Jean, William and Collin are shot in a hail of bullets. Victor will later say that one of the children screamed, "Please don't kill me, I don't want to die." He later says that to him, all the inhabitants of the house didn't look like people; they had the heads of pigs.

The walls were soaked in blood. The killer does not see 4-year-old Phyllis, who is also in the room but hiding.

Evelyn is in the bedroom still clutching the infant in her arms, completely terrified, while her husband lies on the floor below, slowly dying. Evelyn tries to escape from the window together with her baby. She had just managed to get out of the window when Victor hears her and shoots at her. She falls to the ground from the window, still holding the baby.

When Victor goes back into the house and takes another look in the nursery. He finds little Phyllis crouching between the bodies of her two sisters. But he lets her live, because this girl is different from the other children, Victor thinks. Phyllis has the face of an angel. The killer now hears the cry of a baby. He sees baby Larry in the arms of his dead mother. Victor wonders what would happen to the infant now that he no longer has a family. He decides, even though he despises himself for this decision at that moment, to kill the little child as well and shoots the little body.

For Victor, the whole scenario was just like deja vu. He had experienced all this before in a dream. Slowly, panic begins to set in for the 21-year-old. He gathers the shell casings from his rifle and steals seven dollars from the family's wallets. Victor gets back in his car and begins the drive home. What he leaves behind would remain Saskatchewan's most tragic mass murder to this day.

On the way home, Victor is overcome with the thought of now taking his own life. But when he arrives home safely at 7:30 a.m., his father confronts him with the question of where he came from.

Victor's feelings go crazy. Why does he feel so bad now when everything just felt right?

At the same time in Shell Lake, a neighbor is on his way to the Petersons' house. Mr. Lang is waiting outside the house for James, with whom he actually has an appointment.

At about 9:00 a.m., Mr. Lang decides to go check, as the unusual silence in the house makes him suspicious. Right at the entrance, the neighbor finds the body of James Peterson. That's as far as he has to enter the family home to know that something terrible has happened here. He drives to a nearby pay phone and places an emergency call.

Mr. Richards is an officer with the RCMP (Royal Canadian Mounted Police) and is one of the first on the scene. When he enters the house and sees the bodies of the family members, he is visibly surprised to find little Phyllis, still lying between her two sisters, unharmed and, most importantly, alive.

In the bedroom, he finds 5-year-old William, 13-year-old Mary and Collin, only 2 years old, on the mattress. Jean and Pearl are also dead, but crouched between them is 4-year-old Phyllis, unharmed but in shock. The Royal Canadian Mounted Police officer picks the little girl up and takes her to the neighbor's house for the time being, so that she is safe and does not have to continue to be at the scene, where she emerges as the only survivor.

Back in Shell Lake, the officer calls for backup and then returns to the Peterson home.

At the rear of the farmhouse, lying under an open window, he finds the bodies of Evelyn Peterson and baby Larry. The bodies of all the victims have burn marks on them. Burn marks from burn gases caused by a firearm. These so-called "powder burns" only occur when the victim is close to the firing point of the weapon. If the person shot were standing farther away from the barrel of the gun, these gases would quickly dissipate and not cause burns.

The Peterson family has no enemies. Parents Evelyn and James always work hard to provide a carefree life for their children.

The police are now faced with a small number of clues, but they must be linked together as quickly as possible. First, there are the unmistakable bloody footprints on the linoleum. The perpetrator was wearing shoes that had a very specific imprint on the bottom. This was, firstly, a diamond on the sole and a V-shaped image on the heel.

On the other hand, the investigators still find 22 cartridge cases. The perpetrator may have overlooked these in the pressure of time.

Meanwhile, the media reports the incident at the Peterson home, causing panic among residents of Shell Lake and the surrounding area. After all, the killer is still at large and still entirely unknown. Their own family could be the next to be wiped out.

From this point on, the worried residents of Shell Lake only sleep with their lights on and their guns next to their beds in case the killer feels the need to kill again one night. In the media, the night of the crime becomes known as the "Night of Fear."

The RCMP are under tremendous pressure. They don't want to lose any time and want to start investigating as soon as possible so that the population can finally relax. The police have roadblocks set up and are searching the area around the Petersons' house with 75 police dogs. They are asking all surrounding families to report any noticeable items or situations to them immediately. Shoe prints from the crime scene are sent to Regina for forensic testing. After checking the shell casings, it turns out that they would match three different gun models. Since none of the family members escaped except little Phyllis, it is initially assumed there were multiple shooters. No enemies, no signs of robbery or sexual assault suggest that the perpetrator must be someone from the area who drove around and picked a house at random on the night of the crime.

Two days later, on August 17, 1967, a farmer enters the Shellbrooke RCMP saying, "My neighbor's son just got out of the psych ward recently, likes guns and is a good hunter." He gives investigators a name: Victor Ernest Hoffman.

RCMP investigators make their way to the Hoffmans' property in a hurry to question their only suspect about the night of the crime.

Even as they stride to the front entrance of the farmhouse, the first clue emerges. The shoes left outside the door look identical to the ones the perpetrator must have been wearing. The RCMP immediately confiscate them and send them in to be matched with the footprints from the crime scene.

When Victor's father opens the door to investigators, they want to know from him if the family would be in possession of a .22 caliber weapon. Robert Hoffman answers in the affirmative. The gun is also taken into the custody of the RCMP to compare the cartridge cases with those from the crime scene.

It is not 24 hours before investigators receive word that both the shoes and the cartridge cases match those from the night of the crime. There is also blood on the shoes at the time of the seizure, which completely eliminates any doubt about Victor's perpetration.

It was him who attacked and wiped out the family of 9 on the morning of August 15, 1967. Two empty purses are also found on the Hoffmans' property. Both belong to the Peterson family.

On August 19, 1967, four days after the massacre, Victor Hoffman is arrested and taken to the RCMP station for questioning, where after just 15 minutes he confesses to each murder.

He regrets not having burned down the house. That way, the shell casings might not have been found and he might not have been convicted.

The investigator asks Victor if he ever felt the need to commit such a crime. "No, when I was there for a few minutes, it just popped into my head. Do you think I could have gotten rid of the thoughts? No, I just did it then," says Victor.

When asked if he has anything else to say about it, he replies by saying, "No, just that I'm sick in the head. I could never kill anyone again, I'm sure of it."

Victor is arrested the same day.

Over 500 people from Shell Lake and surrounding areas gather at the funeral of the nine victims of the Peterson family as the victims are buried in a mass grave. The only two family members to survive the attack are 19-year-old Cathy, who lives with her husband in British Columbia, and 4-year-old Phyllis, who was spared because she has "an angelic face." At first, little Phyllis is sent to a children's home, for she is now an orphan. Later, however, Cathy and her husband take her in and raise her together.

Despite the terrible event, the small village of Shell Lake and its inhabitants can now breathe a sigh of relief. The perpetrator has been caught and will never be able to harm another human being.

On August 21, 1967, two weeks after the massacre, Victor is transferred to the care of the University Psychiatric Hospital in Saskatoon for an evaluation of his mental condition. The examination at the psychiatric hospital lasts two days.

Victor places part of the blame on the murdered James Peterson: "If he had stayed calm and explained to me that I was wrong, everything would have been okay. He could have helped me, and I wouldn't have killed him, but he tried to stop me." Victor would have been a little scared when he shot James, but not sorry.

He also blames the psychiatric ward in North Battleford. They shouldn't have released him after just three weeks. "If I had had someone to talk to, I wouldn't have committed murder. When I left the psych ward, I knew I was going to kill someone. I'll probably never be able to see the outside world again. I don't know how it all started. I don't know how I started. My head was empty. There was just, "Kill, kill, kill!"

According to him, it was the devil who was partly responsible for the deed. The creature in his head would have deceived him and he could not find a rational explanation why the devil chose him of all people. Victor now wishes to die.

He is again diagnosed with schizophrenia. Despite this, the date for his trial remains. Victor is taken back to Prince Albert Prison after the examination.

The court provides Victor Hoffman with a public defender for his trial. The public defender has 18 years of experience in the field of criminal law, but little experience with mental illness, so he reads a lot about it and requests to see Victor's medical records.

It is confirmed that Victor was suffering from extreme mental illness at the time of the crime.

Victor's lawyer plans to call in several qualified doctors who are familiar with the clinical picture of schizophrenia. And he finds them. Victor's attorney becomes aware of a doctor named

Dr. Abraham Hoffer, who is at the forefront of schizophrenia research. Hoffer is also the co-founder of what is known as the "Hoffer-Osman Diagnostic Test." In this test, various questions are used to differentiate the level of schizophrenia in patients. The average score for a person with this disorder is 65, and when Dr. Hoffer tests Victor for his trial, his score of 99 is striking.

During the tests, Victor tells Dr. Hoffer he doesn't feel guilty. He was just doing what the devil asked him to do. And God would not be angry with him either. He would feel more remorse for stealing guns in his youth than for wiping out the Peterson family. For Dr. Hoffer, Victor is a very special case. In his career as a doctor, he had yet to encounter a patient with as many different perceptions of his surroundings as Victor.

It is the day of Victor's trial.

Dr. Hoffer is called to the stand to give an assessment of Victor's illness. The important thing here is to give the jury an idea of what it's like inside the head of someone suffering from paranoid schizophrenia. "Victor did what he had to do, given the delusions he was suffering from at the time. He had an awareness of what he was doing and felt called to do it."

Other consulted individuals and experts agree that Victor was not completely in control of his actions. He would not have known at the time if what he was doing was wrong. It had not occurred to him to think that way. It is undeniable that Victor shot a family, but the search for a motive is futile, they say.

Victor had been under psychiatric treatment until three weeks before the crime and was considered mentally healthy at that time.

The Canadian Criminal Code states that no one can be held responsible for a crime if they are mentally ill. That Victor committed the crime is beyond question. Only the sentence has yet to be determined, and for that, the defense calls a multitude of experts to the stand.

After three and a half hours of deliberation, the jury finds him not guilty of the murder of the Peterson family.

Victor shows no emotion when it is decided, nevertheless, he should be sent to a psychiatric facility. Only a short time later, Victor is admitted to the Penetanguishene Mental Health Center in Simcoe County, Ontario, where he will now remain for the next three years.

In 1992, book author Peter Tadman conducts an interview with him in which Victor tells him that he would still be hunted and pursued by his nemesis, the devil.

On May 21, 2004, Victor Earnest Hoffman passes away at the age of 56 as a result of cancer.

The only survivor who was present at the "Night of Fear" is Phyllis Peterson. In an interview in the 1990s, she later reveals that the aftermath was an empty and lonely time for her. She sorely misses her family. She has no recollection of the crime itself. "There's really very little that I remember. I remember there were police officers everywhere, but as a kid I didn't understand what exactly was going on," Phyllis said.

Cathy and her husband, along with Phyllis, are moving back to Shell Lake to be close to those they know.

"I had to make a decision. Would I live my life or let Victor 'win.'? He took my family's life. I'm not going to let him take mine, too," Phyllis said of the power Victor had over her even while still in the institution.

...Today, Phyllis is 54 years old and still lives with her husband and son in the small town where her entire family was murdered in 1967.

»What a journey mankind had to make until it reached the point of being gentle even toward the guilty, gentle toward criminals, humane toward the inhumane! Surely it was men of divine nature who first taught this.«

- Johann Wolfgang von Goethe (1749-1832), German poet -

CHAPTER 12

A knife and garlic

Behind the fluttering yellow and black police barrier tape lie numerous, colorful bouquets of flowers. Bound with pink gerberas, yellow lilies and orange chrysanthemums, they rest next to simple bouquets of white roses. Most of the bouquets are still wrapped in cellophane. Snowflakes gently fall from the sky onto the bouquets, gradually covering the colorful plants. Here and there, letters and pictures protected by foil protrude between the bouquets. In the middle of the sea of flowers, a stuffed dog sits next to numerous teddy bears. The wet snow has already soaked the fur of the cuddly toys. The pink pair of ballet shoes and its inscription - someone has written "R.I.P." in black felt-tip pen - seem incongruous to the observer. Here on the side of a road in the Brentwood district, located in the northwest quadrant of the city of Calgary, time seems to stand still.

Again and again, citizens step up to the memorial site and stop. The mourners embrace and comfort each other, while tears run down their cold-reddened cheeks. One or two visitors, on the other hand, can only shake their heads in disbelief. The bewilderment appears to be chiseled into people's faces. Just a few meters from the painful scene, a large number of serious-looking emergency personnel have taken up positions. They closely observe the people who step up to the sea of flowers. Every now and then, the police officers politely ask individuals of the gathered citizens to accompany them to one of their patrol vehicles. The officers are on the lookout for witnesses whose observations may help them reconstruct the gruesome and, to that point, unprecedented event in Canadian criminal history.

Matthew De Grood is a quiet and polite teenager. Although he used drugs in his youth, he never faced any criminal consequences. Upon starting his studies at the University of Calgary, he quickly makes friends with his fellow students, who hold the young man in high esteem. Matthew is a hard-working student. But suddenly the behavior of the once obliging De Grood changes. Matthew begins posting disturbing and increasingly crazy posts on social media. Friends and his sister, who are networked with him on these platforms, do not miss De Grood's strange posts. But the content of the text messages that the dark-haired man sends to his contacts via his cell phone also becomes more threatening each time. The 22-year-old's mother musters all her courage and approaches her son about the disturbing text messages. She tries to explain to Matthew that the wording of the messages and his unpredictable outbursts of rage frighten her. But the woman is not getting through to her child. The student's father also begins to worry about his protégé. Maybe he's using drugs again? There must be a reason why his calm and empathetic boy is gradually turning into a paranoid and distant stranger. The distraught parents ask De Grood's grandfather to address his grandson about his change in nature. The old man is actually Matthew's closest confidant- but he too is not getting through to the boy.

It's April 15, 2014, and the moody month of April lives up to its name - the weather is cold and unstable. As they do every year at the end of the winter semester, the students are having a graduation party. Kaitlin has been looking forward to the social afternoon and the delicious barbecue in the evening. The student, whom her friends also call Kaiti, quickly puts on some subtle makeup before heading to the party, which is to be held at her fellow student's home.

From the beginning of the afternoon until around 9:00 p.m., the thirty something students stay in the large backyard of the house. They take turns gathering around a fire pit to brave the cold; drinking beer and soft drinks. The students laugh and enjoy themselves. They talk about investment and politics to muted music. In the courtyard, two mattresses spray-painted with graffiti invite you to linger. But by 9 p.m., the students find it too uncomfortable to continue partying outside; they head to the home of their fellow student's family.

On graduation day, Matthew has been working his part-time job at a grocery store since 2:00 p.m. when a text message from his old childhood friend Ryan* reaches him. Won't he come to the party, too? Matthew will. Although the young man doesn't actually get off work until 10:00 p.m. and there's still a whole hour to go before then, he leaves his workplace without a word of goodbye. But before he does, Matthew slips a cutter knife into his jacket pocket and shoves a few cloves of garlic into his socks before leaving the store in his work clothes. The disappearance does not go unnoticed by his work colleague, and so she sends him a text message asking where De Grood has just gone? But the woman only receives cryptic text messages back from her colleague.

At a gas station, Matthew meets up with his long-time colleague Ryan. Together, the two students make their way to the party location, which is only a few minutes' walk from their meeting place. De Grood appears very agitated to his childhood friend.

Around 00:30, some of the party guests are drawn back outside to the courtyard to the fire pit, where the burning logs continue to crackle and the blazing fire gives off a cozy warmth. Suddenly, out of the corner of his eye, Charly* notices Matthew placing his cell phone on the blade of an axe lying around. Holding the handle of the tool in his hand, he jerks his cell phone into the rising flames. Charly reflexively grabs the device, whose plastic casing threatens to melt in the blazing flames. In vain, the young man tries to extinguish the phone. But Matthew puts an abrupt end to the attempt when he begins to strike the glowing cell phone that is lying on the ground with an axe. A few axe blows later, the cell phone is completely destroyed. Matthew grabs it and hurls it away. During his outburst of rage, he loudly complains that his parents think he is going crazy. They are constantly getting on his nerves, the student rails; he should seek help and take medication. " No way!" the young man angrily shouts into the night. The guests standing around the fire look in Matthew's direction, startled and embarrassed.

Sometime around this time, Mrs. De Grood receives an alarming text message from her son. "I'm not coming back home," she reads. Panic sweeps through the woman; has Matthew just announced he is going to take his own life? Upset, the mother wakes her son's father and tells him about the disturbing text message. The man jumps out of bed, slips into his pants and puts on a shirt. He quickly reaches for his cell phone and types, "Son, don't do anything rash! We love you!" before shoving the phone into his back pocket and hurrying out of the house to search for his obviously distraught and world-weary child.

Ryan, who invited Matthew to the party, leaves around 1:00 in the morning, along with three other friends, to grab a snack at a well-known fast food chain. After about 20 minutes, the small group returns filled and in a good mood, with provisions in their hands. But as they stroll up the driveway to their fellow student's house, the bloodcurdling screams of a woman put them on alert.

Kaiti. Just a split second later, the front door flies open, and Joshua rushes out of the apartment building. "He's got a knife! Run!" the student yells at his puzzled-looking peers as he runs toward them. The young men are so perplexed that no one is able to even move. The group only starts to move again when their friend looks at them with glassy eyes widened by shock before he collapses bleeding in the front yard of the house. Three of the friends try to save his life. They speak to him and press a piece of clothing onto the gaping wound. Out of the corner of their eyes, the helpers notice a figure rushing out of the house entrance.

While the young men try to save their friend's life, Ryan instinctively rushes after the phantom. In his right hand, the fleeing man holds a knife, its blood-stained blade flashing in the moonlight. Gasping, the figure stops abruptly. Ryan comes to a stop just a few steps behind the other. Adrenaline surges through the young student's veins as the stranger slowly turns to face him. Ryan's limbs startle as he realizes who the attacker is - for a split second, the two men lock eyes. Then Matthew throws the bloodied knife at his friend's feet and sprints off again. Ryan casts only a brief, stunned glance at the red-stained blade before continuing to chase after Matthew. After only a few meters, the young man has almost caught up with his friend when he stops again and turns to face his pursuer. Matthew suddenly reaches into his pocket and pulls out a cutter knife. With the blade extended, Matthew moves toward Ryan, gasping. "Stop following me around. Or you'll be next!" the young man hisses. To add emphasis to his threat, he waves the cutter knife around just inches from Ryan's face. "We're blood brothers after all," Matthew whispers with a sly grin on his face as he wipes his free, bloody hand on his horrified counterpart's jacket. Then Matthew turns and runs off into the night. His friend, who stays behind, decides it's safer for him to return to his fellow student's house.

While Ryan tries to apprehend Matthew, the police receive several 911 calls. Only 5 minutes pass before the first patrol cars arrive on the scene. The officers are confronted with a shocking and confusing scene: students are running back and forth in a panic. At the same time, three young men are trying to give first aid to a person lying on the lawn. The emergency services try to get an overview of the chaos as quickly as possible. From a distance, the rotating rotor blades of an approaching helicopter can be heard, which soon circles over Brentwood, illuminating the darkness of the night with its searchlight.

The emergency forces on the ground receive animal support from a service dog of the dog squadron in their search for the fugitive. The trained animal sniffs out the scent of the fugitive and, barking loudly on command, takes up the pursuit. They quickly get closer and closer to the fugitive. This does not go unnoticed by Matthew, who turns around and confronts his hunters. The officer later reports that the suspect appeared to be attempting a "suicide by cop". However, the officer quickly realizes that his counterpart is unarmed and therefore does not shoot the young man. The policeman issues a command, and the dog immediately charges at Matthew. The animal jumps up at the suspect and bites his arm. But that can't make the enraged boy give up. He whirls his arm, including the dog, through the air; tries to shake off the service dog. But the animal has bitten into Matthew's muscle flesh. In the end, the raging student can do nothing against the police and their service dog - the officers arrest the man at 2:00 a.m., only a few blocks away from the party location and less than an hour after the knife attack. Only a few minutes after the successful arrest, an ambulance arrives at the scene. The paramedics tend to the bloody bite wounds on the man's upper right arm before maneuvering him onto a stretcher and strapping him down. The bright white lights in the ambulance blind Matthew. On the way to the hospital, the wounded man closes his eyes in exhaustion.

Three young men lose the fight for their lives before they can even be taken to a hospital. Morticians wheel their dead bodies out of the house on stretchers, shrouded in black vinyl covers. Two more victims arrive at a nearby hospital with flashing blue lights. It's a race against time. But the young student and her fellow student soon die from their severe injuries.

The officers are quickly able to establish the identity of the arrested man. The young man is 22-year-old student Matthew De Grood. The police officers feel an icy chill run down their spines as they read the name of the alleged perpetrator. One investigator throws his hands up in horror. How the hell are they supposed to tell their former supervisor Douglas, a high-ranking and experienced police officer, that the perpetrator of the gruesome massacre is his own flesh and blood?

The police officers cordon off the scene of the crime with yellow flagging tape, with " Do not cross" emblazoned on it in thick black letters. Startled by the large police contingent in the otherwise quiet and tranquil district, a dozen onlookers and members of the press gradually gather at the police cordon. Soon the work of the forensics team is accompanied by a flurry of flashbulbs from photographing journalists and captured on cameras by filming teams of reporters. The crime scene specialists discover a bloodstained knife - the murder weapon - in the grass. More than 100 police officers are busy with the investigation in the coming days and weeks. Traces have to be secured and analyzed, witnesses questioned and clues to the motive collected.

The day after the horrific murders, Police Chief Rick Hanson holds a press conference. The crime is the worst massacre in Calgary's history, in which five innocent students lost their lives. The veteran investigator's voice keeps failing him as he speaks to members of the press.

In April 2014, the funerals of the slain victims take place. An event that also receives a lot of media attention. Hundreds of people accompany the murdered victims on their last journey. Flags are flown at half-mast throughout the city in honor of the dead.

While an entire city is stunned and grieving, Matthew has recovered from his bite wounds enough to be transferred to a detention center. His parents visit their son regularly in jail until September 2014, when De Grood is transferred to a mental health facility in southern Alberta in Edmonton. After his exploration, an expert witness concludes that the inmate is capable of participating in his trial. Whether the inmate was sane at the time of the murders, however, must be determined during the trial. The public prosecutor's office immediately brought charges of five counts of murder against De Grood.

The trial against the defendant begins in May 2015. Matthew De Grood, now 23, is wearing a plain black suit on the days of the trial. His dark hair is cut short. The courtroom is filled to capacity with trial observers and relatives of the murdered. Every now and then, the defendant sheepishly sips from his water glass. He tries to avoid any eye contact with the people present, especially the relatives of his victims. The party guests tearfully tell the court what they had to go through; of the gruesome images that burned onto their retinas and left them unable to sleep at night.

During the trial, the course of events can be reconstructed with the help of the testimonies of witnesses and experts: It is around 1:00 a.m. in the night when the defendant goes into the kitchen of the house. A wooden knife block sits on an open shelf. Matthew reaches for one of the black knife handles and pulls out a 21 cm long, pointed blade. Gripping the handle of the knife tightly, he turns and stabs Zackariah Rathwell. The unsuspecting student collapses: but his attacker does not let go of him. De Grood stabs the body of his 21-year-old victim seven times. After letting go of

Zackariah, the attacker, the murder weapon still in his hand, walks into the living area of the house.

Joshua, Kaiti and Jordan are sitting below a large window on a comfortable couch, engrossed in a stimulating conversation. And so, they don't notice Matthew approach Jordan before he abruptly stabs him. He then turns to Joshua and critically injures him with several strokes of his knife. Kaiti, sitting next to the two young men during the attack, is paralyzed with fear. It takes several seconds before the young woman can move. While Matthew continues to stab his victim, Kaiti jumps up and tries to escape. The attacker runs after her and catches up with her after a few steps. Then he pushes Kaiti into the corner of the dining room. And slowly walks towards her, with the knife raised. "I'm sorry," Matthew mutters to himself before stabbing the blonde woman over and over again. Her agonized screams can be heard all the way outside.

The attacker's final victim is student Lawrence Hong, who has fallen asleep on a couch. The young man is so sound asleep that he does not notice what is happening around him and that his life is in danger. Matthew bends over his defenseless victim and kills by stabbing him several times as well. While the attacker stands with his back to him, the severely injured Joshua struggles to his feet. With his last strength, he drags himself out of the front door - directly into the arms of Ryan and his friends, who have just organized a food supply at a well-known fast food chain. When Matthew notices the student fleeing, he rushes after him. While Joshua collapses in the front yard fighting for his life, the attacker escapes. Ryan doesn't hesitate much and latches onto his heels.

Even the paramedics who rush to the scene can no longer help the severely wounded student; the blood loss is so great. Still at the scene, they discover the death of Jordan, Lawrence and Zackariah. Joshua and Kaiti lose the fight for survival on the way to the emergency room. After the autopsy, the coroner confirms: the cause of death of all five murder victims is the numerous, severe stab wounds.

During the trial, one of the officers reports what the defendant replied when garlic cloves were found in one of his socks during the body search: he had wanted to ward off vampires and werewolves with it. Three psychiatric experts testified during the trial that Matthew De Grood had suffered from a psychotic delusion at the time of the acts. The young man was delusional and believed that the world would end at midnight and that he would have to fight off his adversaries in the form of vampires and werewolves - his later victims. The experts also note that the mental illness of the accused did not appear suddenly. A psychosis and warning visions, a form of schizophrenia, had already been present in the defendant's mind for several weeks before the crime - apparently the dramatic nature of the illness went unnoticed by those around him. After hearing the expert witnesses, the judge decides that De Grood was not capable of controlling himself at the time of the murders due to his mental illness - the young man cannot therefore be criminally prosecuted for his actions. De Grood is ordered to be placed in the psychiatric ward of the Alberta Hospital in Edmonton. For the relatives of the murder victims, the court's decision is difficult to bear.

Matthew De Grood's defense lawyer, Allan Fay, reads out a statement from his client after the verdict: "I deeply regret that your loved ones are no longer with you. They did not deserve to die. I will work towards regaining the trust of the community."

A family member of one of the victims, on the other hand, states, "The end of this process is not the end of this journey for us, we continue to be broken."

In 2017, after a review, De Grood is given more freedoms and privileges. Under supervision, he is allowed to take walks on the hospital grounds and seek medical treatment from outside medical professionals. It's 2019 when the inmate gets more relaxations.

Matthew is now allowed to leave the clinic on his own and spend the night outside the facility for up to a week. From the evaluators' perspective, De Grood has made very significant progress.

The victims' families, on the other hand, are very concerned about the relaxations. They fear De Grood could suffer another psychotic episode, causing great suffering to even more people. In Canadian law, it is not De Grood who must prove that he is no longer a risk to himself and his fellow human beings, but the state that must present evidence that the inmate is still a danger to society. Three times a year, a decision may be made whether the convict must remain in the secure facility or whether he will be released. Each time, the bereaved families anxiously await the decision of the evaluator in charge.

The house with the tragic story has meanwhile been sold. A young man bought the small building painted white and blue. The new owner promises to maintain a small outdoor memorial in honor of the victims - five lit candles and five fresh bouquets of flowers. On the tree at the small memorial hangs a laminated white note with pictures of the victims and their names along with a text that concludes, "...they will never be forgotten, and they shall find rest and peace." Right next to the front door of the house where the horrible massacre happened in 2014, leans a wooden sign painted white, with four large letters written one below the other in red paint- HOPE.

** Some names have been changed.*

No matter how much evil may multiply, it can never completely cancel out the good.

- Thomas Aquinas (1225-1274), Italian philosopher and theologian -

CHAPTER 13

Enough is enough

Karl feels elated. And that's despite the fact that he's on his way to work. The sun has only just risen on this March 12, 1982, but today is Friday - the long-awaited weekend is just around the corner. Even the early start in the morning can't dampen the young man's good mood. Karl strolls down the street with an almost bouncing gait and whistling to himself. He enjoys the fresh, cool morning air; the first, warming rays of sunlight kissing his face and the wonderful peace of the surroundings. On this road, at this early hour, one rarely encounters other pedestrians or motorists. Karl is all the more surprised when he sees a car parked at the side of the road from a distance. The closer the man gets to the car, the slower he walks. A large pool of blood can be seen on the pavement. "Has there been an accident here?" he murmurs and looks around in a questioning manner. Once at the car, Karl peers through the driver's window into the interior of the jeep, his heart pounding. Shocked, the boy turns away from the vehicle before sprinting down the street the next moment-he has to get help fast.

On January 25, 1949, a little girl is born in the suburban community of Brooklyn, located in Queens County in the Canadian province of Nova Scotia. Her parents Morris and Gladys Hurshman christen their second child Jane Marie. Two more offspring follow in the coming years. The Hursmans' daughter is a petite child who is always polite and friendly to those around her. At school she shines with her diligence and enthusiasm for reading. And she loves to do sports. The girl with the soft and thoughtful voice grows up to be a smart and hardworking young woman who learns two foreign languages in addition to her native tongue. While Jane is still a toddler, her father joins the Canadian Army to fight in the Korean War. After his service, he returned to his family in 1952. But the soldier remains loyal to the military, and in 1954 the Hurshman's receive orders from the Army to move to the town of Truro. One of many moves to follow.

At this time, father Morris becomes addicted to alcohol. The man begins to drink more and more excessively. Soon the consequences of consumption become noticeable: The war returnee becomes increasingly irritable, and his mood begins to fluctuate greatly. Sometimes the family man is overcome by such rage that he becomes downright angry. Not only does he constantly argue with his wife Gladys; he often gives vent to his anger against his mother in a physical way. Not infrequently, Jane wakes up at night because of their loud quarrels. The frightened girl then hides under her blanket and prays that the argument will pass quickly. If her younger siblings wake up due to the commotion, her big sister comforts them and talks them into courage. Even though the father of the family never lays a hand on his children, the nightly quarrels increasingly traumatize the siblings. For the children, violence and alcohol soon become part of normality: all of the father's friends also drink and scuffle. "Men seem to be like that," his children think to themselves.

With the Cold War between the Western powers and the Eastern bloc raging since 1947, the military summons Morris, along with his family, to Germany in 1957. The Hurshmans take up residence in an apartment building with a pub selling cheap beer across the street. The father of the family now no longer has any control over his alcoholism. The man loses his temper more and more often. The physical and mental abuse of his wife becomes more brutal. And even the children fall victim to his tirades of abuse.

It is 1964 when the army decides that the family should move to Canada again. This time the Hurshmans move to Winnipeg, capital of the province of Manitoba. Jane is now 15 years old. After living abroad for so long, moving back to her home country makes the teen lonely. When a Hurshman family friend is ordered back to Jane's native province of Nova Scotia by the military, the girl senses her chance to escape loneliness. She begs her parents to allow her to accompany the other family-just for the summer. Morris and Gladys allow their daughter to travel; they have no idea that their girl will never return to her parents' home.

Jane does not feel comfortable with the other family after only a few days. The couple is always drunk and fighting loudly; the husband constantly beats up his wife. The teenager therefore can no longer bear it there and comes to live with her grandmother in Liverpool. Here the 15-year-old meets Milford Whynot, 9 years her senior. Milfie, as his friends call him, seems interested in the young girl. The young man is not violent, which impresses Jane. Shortly after her 16th birthday, Jane learns that she has become pregnant by Milfie. The father-to-be seems to want to take responsibility. Jane leaves school to take on her new responsibilities as a housewife and mother. Then, on April 25, 1965, the wedding bells ring. The newlyweds move into the home of Milford's grandparents. But this decision soon puts a strain on the young marriage, and Jane and Milfie move into a small cottage of their own. During their time together, Jane gives birth to two healthy boys: first Alan is born; little Jamie follows in 1972. But the birth of her second son is very traumatic for the young woman: she loses enough blood to even require a blood transfusion. After her recovery, doctors urgently advised the mother of two against another pregnancy - the risk was too high and the consequences possibly life-threatening.

Milford drinks more and more frequently until he develops an alcohol addiction. The drug soon dominates his daily life, and the young family man loses his job. The more her husband declines, the more ambitious Jane starts to become. She wishes for a different, a better life. In September 1970, the 21-year-old takes a course to catch up on her school-leaving certificate and a typing course to improve her chances on the job market.

Jane is unhappy in her marriage; even the birth of her second son cannot mend her parents' bond. More and more often she thinks about leaving Milfie. She only draws strength for a separation when she befriends the tall, beefy Billy Stafford, a buddy of Milford. The young man encourages her in her plan to separate from the father of her children.

Billy's real name is Lamont William; but only the cops and judges call him that. Stafford frequently runs afoul of the law. He openly threatens the officers to shoot them if they ever dare to set foot in his house. If a dangerous person approach to Stafford cannot be avoided, the police officers are instructed to always show up at Billy's house with two men. Without further ado, the protective police officers trust the notorious bully to simply shoot them down when he feels like it. The 34-year-old has been violent since he was a child. A childhood friend even says Billy was "sadistic" even as a young boy. Stafford was born on February 13, 1941, the second child of Winnie and Lamont. Over the years, Billy had three more siblings. After his parents gave birth to three girls and two boys, they decided to provide a home for an orphan. The children were raised without compromise. For example, Lamont is said to have once burned his son Billy's hand to teach him not to steal. The older the boy gets, the more brutal he becomes. The ruffian now doesn't even stop at his parents; his father in particular is intimidated by the stocky boy, who at 1.83 m soon weighs 115 kg.

The 21-year-old Billy marries his first wife Pauline in 1962, but it doesn't take long for Stafford to show his true colors. He maltreats the young woman whenever he feels like it - with beer bottles, broomsticks and with his bare fists he beats his defenseless partner. Billy is unpredictable. Whether he is drunk or not, from one second to the next, the previously friendly man can turn into a raging beast with hateful eyes and frothing at the mouth for no reason. During their marriage, Pauline gives birth to five children. They, too, suffer from their father's violence. When their mother manages to finally separate from the domestic tyrant, his offspring are so severely traumatized that they fall silent and no longer speak a word. Billy, meanwhile, does not mourn his family for long. He soon meets a new woman. Faith, too, quickly finds herself in different circumstances. She gives birth to a baby boy, whom she names Rodney. Her parents took the young mother to another town before her first child was born, to protect her from the violent Stafford.

All of Bangs Falls trembles when Billy, who makes his living as a sailor, gets into his car-not infrequently drunk or drugged. These trips often end in accidents, but even the repeated revocation of his driver's license can't stop Stafford from getting behind the wheel. Billy owns an arsenal of guns and is known in the area as an accomplished deer hunter. He does not have a hunting license. Still, Stafford always has a rifle in his truck. Every time he sees a deer while driving around, he kills the animal. Even outside the hunting season and without observing the fixed shooting quota. No rules or laws apply to him.

It is 1975 when Jane gives her husband an ultimatum: either his wife and sons or alcohol. Milford opts for the bottle. Jane packs her bags and moves out with 3-year-old Jamie. 10-year-old Alan wants to stay with his father-although his mother doesn't approve of the decision, she agrees to her son's wishes. Jane temporarily lodges in a friend's apartment with Jamie. In the coming weeks, the wife urges her husband to finally agree to the divorce. In January of 1976, the time has come: Milfie signs the divorce papers. But not without setting his condition: the father demands that his sons Alan and Jamie stay with him. Jane is torn. However, she now believes that she has found the man of her dreams in Billy Stafford. He sweeps the young woman off her feet, gives her gifts and promises to always be by her side and protect her. The sailor is loving and understanding to the petite woman with the soft voice. She now wants to invest all her strength and time in the new relationship - and so she leaves her children with their father.

The couple soon moves into a small cottage and Jane takes Billy's last name- but without being formally married. As with Stafford's previous relationships, he is unable to hide his true self for long with Jane. A rift occurs when the man discovers birth control pills lying on his girlfriend's pillbox. Jane tries to explain to her upset partner why she depends on birth control: another pregnancy could be fatal for her. "You're out of your mind! Let nature take its course!" he yells, firing the blister of hormone pills out an open window in a high arc. After that, the subject of preventing conception is over for him.

Only a few weeks later, Jane is shocked to discover that she is bearing new life under her heart. The further the pregnancy progresses, the ruder Stafford behaves towards his partner. He drinks copious amounts of alcohol and insults Jane at every opportunity because of her pregnancy-related weight gain. Billy seems increasingly ashamed of his girlfriend, as he no longer shows himself in public with her.

It is May of 1976 when Jane gives birth to a baby boy, whom she christens Darren. The mother barely survives the birth. Doctors advise her to undergo sterilization to avoid future pregnancies. Against Billy's will, she agrees to the procedure. In addition to the disappointment that Jane did not give him a girl, Stafford is furious with his partner's decision to become infertile. Not once does he visit the new mother and his now sixth son at the clinic or inquire how his little family is doing. Now that Jane can no longer get pregnant, she is of no interest to Stafford.

After a few days in the hospital, the mother and the little infant are discharged. The doctors implore the woman to take it easy for the next few weeks and not to do any heavy lifting-otherwise she risks rupturing the surgical stitches. When Jane returns home after her hospital stay, she can't believe her eyes. Billy has been in the rooms like an animal during her absence and has destroyed all the furniture. Jane hasn't even taken off her jacket, put down her travel bag, and taken care of little Darren when Stafford orders her to clean up his mess and clean thoroughly. There is no running water in the couple's home; the cleaning bucket can only be filled at a fountain. Billy refuses to help his son's new mother with this. He doesn't care what the doctors have advised Jane to do.

Once Stafford is back at sea, Jane visits his parents Lamont and Winnie. She laments her suffering to them; reports how badly her son is treating her. The woman is hopeful that Billy's mother and father might be talking to him. But Lamont refuses. She should see things from the perspective of the father of six. He first has to get used to sharing the attention of his partner, whom he has long had to himself, with an infant. His advice: she should just give his son some time.

A few days later, Jane heads to the clinic to have the stitches from the surgery removed. The same evening Billy returns from the sea and directly demands sex from his partner. She tries to explain that the doctors advised her not to have sex in the coming weeks because the scars have not fully healed. Even now, Stafford is not interested in what the doctors think is best for Jane. He orders her to take off her clothes. As the woman stands before him exposed, he mocks her body, scarred by the rigors of pregnancy and sterilization. With his huge hands, Billy grabs Jane's sensitive breasts and begins to knead them firmly between his fingers before trying to squeeze out some breast milk with all his might to drink from them. He is not interested in his partner's pained sighs. He pushes her onto the marital bed before brutally raping her.

It is August of 1977 when the landlord throws Jane and Billy out of his house along with their 4 week old baby Darren. To make matters worse, the father of the family loses his job for beating up his captain after an argument. But the family is lucky: one of their friends owns a piece of land. On it is a small cabin in the woods, which he leaves to the homeless family. A few days later, Stafford learns that he also got away scot-free with the beating attack on the skipper. The police investigate, but possible witnesses refuse to testify - the fear of the brutal sailor Billy is too great.

Stafford now receives unemployment benefits and therefore allows Jane to look for a job to supplement the living for the small family. The young mother finds employment as a cook in an old people's home. Her earned wages, which the family does not need for daily needs, are clawed by Billy, who wastes all the money. When Jane wants to keep some of her pay for herself, Stafford freaks out.

Over the next few weeks, Billy's aggression continues to increase-until he beats up his partner for the first time. In November 1977, he believes he observed Jane flirting with his friend Richard. The hooligan yanks her hair and calls her a whore. He is out of his mind as he lashes out at the petite woman, punching and kicking her. Driven by his jealousy, the beating attacks on Jane are repeated more and more often. Billy considers the woman his property; orders her what to do and what not to do and watches her every step of the way. In a drugged stupor, he tortures his partner over three days by tying her to a chair, threatening his hostage with a loaded firearm, and urinating on the defenseless woman. But it is not only the physical attacks of the brawny man that continue to increase Jane has to let him humiliate her by making her drink his urine, putting a dog collar on her and raping her over and over again.

But it is not only Jane who suffers from Stafford's violence; her son Darren also has to put up with his father's beatings and humiliations on a regular basis since his earliest months of life. He abuses the boy so severely that Darren regularly has bruises and bloody wounds. At one point, Billy beats the child so severely that he cokes himself. Stafford urges Darren to stuff food into himself as fast as he can until he vomits-then Billy forces him to eat his vomit. He even threatens the toddler with knives and firearms. Stafford's son has learned to endure the agony of abuse without making a sound. He knows that every cry of pain encourages his producer to beat him even harder. When Stafford has had his way with the toddler, he forbids Jane to comfort the boy. When the mother does find the courage to intervene, Billy beats her up too. The ruffian feels no empathy or compassion for any living creature. Even the two family dogs are tortured and beaten by their master whenever he gets the chance.

All the cruelties that take place in the Stafford house do not remain hidden from neighbors, acquaintances and relatives. But no one dares to help Jane and her young son for fear of incurring the wrath of Billy Stafford.

Meanwhile, Jane's sons from her first marriage still live with their father Milfie. But 15-year-old Alan, in the midst of puberty, begins to rebel. It is October of 1980 when the teenager receives a suspended sentence for breaking into a house. Milford is so overwhelmed with raising the rebel that the boy henceforth lives with his mother and her brutal live-in boyfriend.

Alan is sent to a school that specializes in helping children and adolescents with behavioral problems. In August 1981, the teachers are so satisfied with the teenager's social behavior and academic performance that he is able to attend a regular school again. The boy moves back in with his biological father. But the peace does not last long. Soon Alan commits the next crime. The youth welfare services ask Jane to take in her son again, but the mother refuses. It is the violent Billy, who advocates that the rebel move back in with the Staffords. What the boy thinks of the decision can only be guessed at. One day, however, the teenager steals a car and plans to take his own life by driving across the harbor wharf into the cold sea. But the police catch him in the act of theft and thus unknowingly thwart his suicide. As a result, the distraught teen confides in his mother. "Mom, we are not alive. We are not alive. We are merely robots. We only exist," he reveals to Jane the inner emptiness he feels, which robs him of the courage to live.

The distress and hopelessness in her son's eyes break Jane's heart and gives her the final push: "Enough is enough!" the battered woman repeats to herself mantra-like one night. Then she slips out of the marital bed, grabs a rifle, loads it and points it at the snoring Billy. With trembling hands, she holds the barrel to the bully's temple. "Shit!" hisses Jane, putting the gun back down. Before she can pull the trigger, her mother's heart speaks up, "Do you really want your 4-year-old son to see the mess you made when you blew his father's brains out? Darren will break from that." No, she doesn't. They've all suffered enough as it is. Over the next few days, Jane is overcome again and again with the need to end her torment and her children's martyrdom. She doggedly considers what to do to escape all this. In desperation, she even considers taking her own life - but what will happen to little Darren? She can't possibly leave him with his tyrannizing father. Alan, on the other hand, would be old enough to take care of himself. Or... she could kill Darren and Alan first, before putting the gun in her own mouth. But the very thought of taking the lives of her beloved sons that she once gave them leaves the mother with a heavy heart. “No. I want my children to live. Billy must die!” she thinks to herself resolutely. But her plan to hire a hit man cannot be implemented - the man she has chosen for the job keeps refusing.

It’s March 11, 1982, an ordinary Thursday at the Stafford home. Before Billy gets back to building a pigsty on the property, he rapes Jane. Then she has to do the housework that needs to be done while he turns his attention to his work outside. But neighbor Margaret accosts the man: no way does she want the smelly pigsty next to her property. The two homeowners get into a loud argument: Billy yells at the woman and hurls crude expletives at her. Margaret, well aware of her neighbor’s brutality, backs off to get out of the line of fire of Billy’s tantrum. She goes to Jane and urges her to speak to the troublemaker again and dissuade him from building the pigsty. The young woman has to muster all her courage to take her partner up on it. But she has no choice. Otherwise, a nasty neighbor dispute would ensue, that much is clear. As she expected, Billy, approached about the construction, flips out and takes his anger out on Jane, as he often does.

The family man’s without-a-fault bad mood plummets to zero when he stomps up to Jane later in the day and demands money from her. When they do not comply with his appeal, because otherwise the upcoming contribution for the car insurance cannot be paid, Billy grabs the freshly washed laundry and rumbles outside. He throws the clean clothes into the mud and rolls them in it. When he is satisfied with his work, Stafford brings the dirty laundry back into the house to the frightened mother. The bully is so enraged that he beats the defenseless woman over and over again, expressing his contempt for her by spitting on her while Jane writhes in pain on the floor. He then takes the last of the family's money from her purse. Together with buddy Ronnie, who has been staying at the Stafford house for a while, Billy drives away.

As soon as Jane hears the sound of the SUV's engine die away in the distance, she picks herself up off the ground. Her limbs ache with every movement. Resigned, she picks up the mud-covered clothes and washes them again. Early in the evening, Billy and Ronnie return home- drunk and befuddled from the high of marijuana. Stafford orders Jane to play chauffeur for the two men that evening. First, she is to drive them to a buddy's house. Halfway there, Billy dictates to his girlfriend to stop. Together with Ronnie, the man gets out of the car and rolls a joint. Pulling on the marijuana cigarette with relish, passing the bag back and forth in turn, the men stand on the side of the road. Jane, meanwhile, sits still and slumped in the driver's seat. In her mind's eye, the disturbing images of the abuse and torture she and her children have endured over the years flash before her; she sees the pain and despair in Darren and Alan's eyes. The longer she is lost in thought, the more the tormented woman realizes that she and her children would never be able to escape Billy. Abruptly, Jane is jolted out of her dark thoughts when the doors of the Jeep are yanked open, and the two intoxicated men re-enter the SUV.

Arriving at the mate's house, the two men disappear inside while the distraught woman is left in the car. Hour after hour passes as the friends play cards and drink alcohol. Eventually, the front door slams open and out stagger Billy and Ronnie. The men join the waiting Jane in the car. She is now to take the buddies home. On the drive, Billy slurs to himself that he bought gas and plans to set the neighbor's house on fire. He is already looking forward to watching the flames raze Margaret's home to the ground. Then he turns to Jane. His alcoholic breath hits her as he announces in a threatening tone, "And your wayward son Alan will be taken care of!"

Arriving at the Stafford house, Ronnie jumps out of the jeep and staggers into the house. Left behind is Jane with Billy, who is sleeping it off in the passenger seat. She listens to his heavy, alcohol-smelling breath and the snoring sounds. Getting out of the car, the woman is not allowed to follow one of Billy's strange rules: Jane must stay in the car until her boyfriend has slept off his intoxication and gives her permission to go inside.

Jane looks at the drunk and sinks back into her dark thoughts. "Enough is enough," she whispers to herself again before tentatively pressing the horn of the Jeep. She hopes to catch Alan's attention, but he doesn't respond. The boy thought that Billy must have attacked his mother again and accidentally hit the horn. But when a warning signal sounds again, the teenager decides to go outside the door to see what's going on.

He catches sight of his mother sitting stock-still at the wheel of the SUV, carefully rolling down the driver's window. Billy continues to sit beside her, asleep. The boy walks over to his mother. "Alan," she whispers, "you have to do what I tell you now. Run and get me a rifle-loaded." Without asking a question, the teen hurries back into the house and returns with a shotgun. He hands the gun to his mother, who has snuck out of the car and is now standing next to the closed driver's door. "Get back inside," she orders Alan, who immediately obeys.

With the shotgun in her trembling hands, she points the barrel of the gun at Stafford's head through the rolled-down driver's window. She can't look and turns her face to the side. Before pulling the trigger, she takes a deep breath and presses her eyes and mouth together tightly. The crack of the gunshot shatters the silence of the night. A few seconds later, Alan is standing in the front door again, gazing at the scenario: his bloodied mother holding the shotgun and the Jeep, its interior hidden by windows speckled with blood and shredded tissue. Jane doesn't know if Billy is dead, she just hopes he is. But to look at what she has done - she does not dare. And so, she cannot suspect that she has decapitated Stafford with just one shot.

Cool as a robot, the self-made widow just functions. She instructs her son to fetch her clean clothes. Jane stuffs the blood-stained laundry into a garbage bag and tosses it into the back of the SUV. The shotgun is to be taken by Alan to neighbor Margaret-roommate Roger will help him make the gun disappear. She also asks the teen to call his grandpa, her father Morris. Jane tells her son a place and a time for Morris to wait for her.

While Alan sets about completing the tasks assigned to him, the killer joins her victim in the jeep. She does not dare to even glance to the side. She starts the car and drives to the place 15 km away where she has summoned her father. Under no circumstances should the car stop in front of her house- the danger is too great that Darren will discover his dead father.

When she arrives at the meeting place, the woman parks the car on the side of the road and gets out of the blood-stained vehicle. She reaches for the garbage bag in the back of the truck before seeing her parents' car appear on the horizon just a short time later. Wordlessly, the young woman climbs into the car with Morris and Gladys. "What happened to you?!" the two look at their daughter, startled. "Please don't ask me," she replies, exhausted, before Morris starts the car and drives off.

Arriving at her parents' house, Jane slips into the bathtub filled with soothing hot water. After cleaning her body, she gets out of the tub and stuffs her dirty clothes into the garbage bag with the other bloodstained clothes. Then she asks her father to drive her home.

Once there, she finds a note from Alan on the kitchen table; he is with Margret. Jane goes into the bedroom and flicks the light on and off in quick succession to signal her neighbor that she has returned home. Just a few minutes later, Margret, along with roommate Roger and Jane's son Alan, are at the Staffords' front door. Jane is grateful that her neighbors aren't asking pesky questions. And that little Darren hasn't woken up from all the commotion. Neither has Billy's friend Ronnie, who lies unconscious on the couch sleeping it off.

Alan and his mother set about burning the blood-stained clothes. As the blazing flames consume the laundry, the teenager tells them that he and Roger broke the murder weapon into three pieces and dumped it in a nearby river.

Late that night, Jane settles into her bed. But she does not find sleep. Waves of panic flood her mind as she thinks that Billy might still be alive and might return. For that would undoubtedly be her death sentence-and surely that of her sons.

As the morning of the next day dawns, Jane pays a visit to her neighbor. On her way back home, she sees a patrol car pull up the driveway. Her heart beats so fast she fears it might jump out of her chest. Two police officers get out of the car and walk up to Jane, who can't move for fear. The officers were called to a vehicle parked on the side of the road that morning. The clerk, Karl, made a gruesome discovery in the car. The windshield and passenger window are speckled with blood and tissue shreds. In the passenger seat, a severely injured man appears to be sitting in a lake of blood-so significantly wounded that the young man can barely recognize him as a human creature. Karl immediately realizes at the sight of the scene: the person must be dead. He rushes to call the police. In the parked car, they discover the body of murdered 41-year-old violent offender Lamont William Stafford, whom everyone just called "Billy." When questioned at the scene, no one claims to have seen or heard anything that night. Now it is up to the police officers to deliver the death news to the murdered man's partner. Jane collapses unconscious in front of the officers. At this point, the officers have no idea that it is pure relief, not shock at Stafford's death, that momentarily robs the petite woman of consciousness. Gently, the men carry Billy's partner into the house and lay her on the couch.

Billy's body is taken for forensic examination. The medical examiners document a bullet wound just below the dead man's left ear. The muzzle of the gun appears to have been only about six inches from the victim's head when the shot was fired. Ten homicide investigators are busy trying to solve Stafford's murder. It soon crystallizes that Billy's partner, in particular, is a suspect in the man's murder. They learn of domestic violence at the Stafford's home and that Billy has a life insurance policy worth $20,000 (about 14. 750 GBP). When the officers discover that this is the exact amount of money Jane repeatedly offered a fisherman to kill her partner, it is time for the homicide investigators to pay a visit to Widow Stafford.

In the darkness of March 13, 1982, just one day after the dead man was found in the jeep, a police unit is outside the Stafford home-armed with a search warrant-around midnight. While some of the officers begin searching the property, two officers take Jane to the local police station. They produce photographs of the woman. In the process, the officers notice numerous injuries on the petite body; hematomas in every color imaginable to deep black cover the body of her counterpart.

After several hours of interrogation, the battered woman asks to speak to her father-in-law Lamont, Billy's father. The homicide investigators agree; they hope the suspect will reveal herself to the old man. When Lamont arrives at the station, he sits down with Jane. A homicide investigator discreetly stands in a corner of the room to listen to the conversation. Quietly, Lamont asks, "Did you kill

Billy?" Jane looks down at the floor and swallows. Then she whispers a soft "Yes." Then the dam is broken. After the officers talk to the woman about her motive, record her murder confession, and inspect the crime scene together, one of the cops says to his colleague, "If you ask me, the woman deserves a medal."

For 12 hours Jane is at the police station until the policemen take her home so she can get some rest. Exhausted, the woman falls into her bed and closes her eyes. She feels 4-year-old Darren crawl into bed with her. She strokes the little boy's hair as he snuggles against her chest. Then she whispers into the silence, "I killed your father...". She swallows as she anxiously waits for the little boy's reaction. "I'm glad," is the only thing Darren says. Relieved, his mother kisses him on the forehead before they both fall into a deep sleep.

Prosecutors charge the 33-year-old with Stafford's murder. On November 02, 1982, the trial begins. After 18 days of trial, the jury reaches a verdict that Jane should be acquitted. All the trial observers present stand up and applaud the jury for their decision. But Jane's attorney dampens their relief; he is certain that the prosecution will appeal this verdict. Prosecutors argue that Jane had no right to murder him, despite her domestic situation and the fact that Billy was a bad person.

Immediately after the verdict is announced, Jane sets out to visit her sister, who has been taking care of little Darren while she has been in custody. In early December 1982, the mother moves to Ontario with her boy to get some distance. But only a short time later, the two return to Bangs Falls. There, Jane begins training to become a nursing assistant. Meanwhile, the prosecution successfully challenged the verdict. Prosecutors and defense attorneys negotiate a plea deal whereby Jane receives a prison sentence of 6 months and probation of 2 years for manslaughter- the prosecution wants to set an example to deter other people in similar situations from committing such acts as a supposed act of liberation. While the convict is serving her sentence at the Halifax Correction Center, she is allowed to attend her nursing assistant classes with an escort so that she can successfully complete the training. After the woman has served 2 months of her sentence, she is pardoned and released from prison.

After her release from prison, the 35-year-old applies for a name change for herself and son Darren; from now on, both bear Jane's maiden name: Hurshman. Further difficult years follow for the mother, because even if Billy can no longer torment her and her children, she still suffers from the mental wounds inflicted on them by the tyrant. Jane only barely survives a suicide attempt. She only regains her confidence and courage to face life again when the now 40-year-old woman meets the mechanic, Joel Corkum. Soon the newly in love couple buys a house and a short time later the wedding bells ring in October 1991.

Jane has made it her mission to give lectures on domestic violence and to stand by abused women. Her commitment is not met with goodwill by everyone - only two months after her marriage, the woman receives threatening messages. For example, in addition to a note with the words, "Hello bitch, I just want you to know I haven't forgotten about you!" slipped under the windshield wiper of her car, she also receives a call at her parents' home. The caller threatens, "I just want you to know that I always know where you are." Jane takes the threats very seriously. The mother informs the police. The woman is afraid that someone is trying to kill her. Sons Alan and Jamie are grown and can now fend for themselves. She makes arrangements for Darren, now 15, should something happen to her.

It is the morning of February 22, 1992, nearly 10 years after Billy's death, when a dead woman is found in a parked car on the Halifax lakefront, having died under mysterious circumstances.

Except for the driver's door, all other doors of the car are locked. The dead woman is sitting in the driver's seat; her upper body has slumped to the passenger side. A gun is lying in her lap. A bullet wound is visible in the woman's chest area. Officers discover a sealed envelope in the dead woman's left jacket pocket. The officers open it and pull out a note: "Now you don't talk anymore. I got you!" Who wrote the messages, which read like messages from Billy from beyond the grave, is still not clear.

After intensive research, experts assume that it was a suicide - even though the extensive investigations have not ruled out with absolute certainty that 42-year-old Jane Hurshman Corkum was murdered.

Closing words of the author

Dear Reader,

I hope that the short stories presented have moved you as much as they moved me while writing them. Let us all go through the world with attentive eyes for the needs of others, hopefully preventing many more tragedies.

Did you enjoy the book? If so, may I ask you one final favour? Authors, especially independent ones, need reviews, otherwise they won't be found on the incredibly large digital marketplace.

My dream is to dedicate a book to every country in the world and to collect the most spectacular True Crime cases for you. With only 5 minutes of your time and a positive review, you will help me to realize this dream.

Now right after the audio book is finished, you have the opportunity to do so.

I thank you in advance and wish you all the best

Yours Adrian Langenscheid

Instagram: @truecrimedeutschland

RECOMMENDATIONS

Some of the most famous German podcasts have contributed to this book. If you speak German, I highly recommend any of the following podcasts.

UK TRUE CRIME

UK True Crime, hosted by Adam, is one of my favourite UK podcasts. Since 2016, there has been a new episode every Tuesday. The podcast also discusses lesser known British crime cases. Each episode is presented in a very likeable and down-to-earth way. The cases are varied in selection, very well researched, factually accurate and respectfully narrated in tone. If you don't know the podcast yet, then that should definitely change.

TRUE CRIME INTERNATIONAL:

The successful book series by Adrian Langenscheid

His distinctive style and the success of his books made Adrian Langenscheid one of the most successful true crime authors in Germany. Did you like this book? Then feel free to order the other books in the series.

Made in United States
Troutdale, OR
11/28/2023

15094664R00131